S0-FJO-434

Movement and Creative Drama for Children

Movement and Creative Drama for Children

BETTY LOWNDES

Plays, Inc. *Boston*

First published in Great Britain 1971 under the title
Movement and Drama in the Primary School
First American edition published by Plays, Inc. 1971

Library of Congress Catalog Card Number 73-130840
ISBN 0-8238-0121-7

Printed in Great Britain
for the publishers
Plays, Inc, Boston, Mass. 02116

Contents

Acknowledgment

Grateful thanks are given to Miss E. W. Tout, the Head teacher whose planning and foresight provides a unique teaching environment in which it is a pleasure to work.

Thanks are also due to other members of staff Mrs D. De Gaute, Mrs A. Luckett and Miss Tanner for helpful advice and co-operation.

Particular thanks to Ernest Bowker for his constant help and encouragement, and to Douglas Lowndes who took some of the photographs.

Thanks are also due to the many children who took part in the various improvisations; and to Jeannie Robb and Ann Power.

Special thanks are due to Thelma M. Nye of Batsford for her constructive advice, helpful criticism and patience.

B.L.

London 1970

Introduction

One of the dominant features in Primary Education today is the change in attitude to the role which expressive movement and drama have to play in the development of young children. Three main principles are involved:

1 The increasing awareness of children as children.
2 The re-appraisal of new educational methods leading to the integrated day in the primary school.
3 Research into the fundamental nature of education that has led to the realisation that children must want to learn if a true educational process is to be established.

Movement and drama naturally encompass these three principles, as they allow the children to be children and to express their own personalities. The flexibility of the subjects make an easy starting area for the exploration of other disciplines and there is no easier way to make children want to learn than through play and improvisation.

This book is a description of the movement and drama work carried out in an infants' school in North London based on these three principles. It is offered as a series of suggestions to young teachers who wish to work in a freer expressive way. It is, however, only a series of suggestions and, as such, the exercises should be used as the starting points from which the teacher can then develop her own approach.

The basic aim of the book is to help the teacher to get started, in the belief that once the teacher gains confidence in herself and the children, her experience in the classroom will be as pleasurable and rewarding as it is to the author.

The book consists of six 'work' chapters, each covering one aspect of movement and drama. This division is mainly for easy reference but much of the work would of course have to be interlinked in response to the needs of the children.

These work chapters are preceded by two chapters on the educational elements involved. The first establishes a broad picture of what is meant by movement and drama, under two headings, *What is movement thinking?* and *What is creative drama?* The second chapter defines the role of the teacher and then outlines the capability range of the children aged five to nine. The teacher must have a clear grasp of these two elements if her work is to meet with success.

1 Movement and drama

What is movement thinking?

Laban said that 'Movement thinking could be considered as a gathering of impressions of happenings in one's own mind for which nomenclature is lacking. This thinking does not serve orientation in the external world but it perfects men's orientation in his inner world in which impulses continually surge and seek an outlet in doing, acting and dancing'.

It is interesting to compare this concept with Ouspensky's belief that there are emotional and movement centres in the human being which control man's involuntary and impulsive actions, and that movement thinking is therefore, in part, an orientation of these points of control which are outside the normal conscious and mental levels of thought . . . and which are very much part of primitive tribal life.

These two separate beliefs indicate that 'movement thinking' is concerned with the process that is the heightening and perfecting of a conscious awareness of an external experience in the moment that it is assimilated in the unconscious, and then immediately reacted upon. Because of this inter-relation to all kinds of experience (visual, sensual, auditory, oral, emotional) it allows for a wider expression of personality than conventional modes, involving words and written statements. Education which is concerned primarily with written expression and verbal thought can be limiting and can, in fact, restrict the mental development of young people. Children learn a great deal by movement, which gives them an understanding of space, both the kinesphere (space immediately surrounding the body) and outer general space (space in the region beyond the kinesphere) which is shared by other people as well as by self. Feeling and sight come to be related, and a sense of judgment and scale become reality.

Emotional expression is more easily manifested through action. A young child will not hesitate to show his happiness or anger both by mouth and limb movements. In fact, the essence of communication is gestural, involving facial expression and body movement. This is clearly evident in eastern countries where, for example, the Balinese theatre is communicated mainly through gesture and movement. The accent on verbal expression in the western world has not allowed for this wider development. Similarly, restrictions were placed on the visual arts (by the Renaissance) which were only released after the Impressionists discovered the freer concepts of Japanese painting. At the same time *avant garde* theatre began to involve the idea of movement and gesture as a necessary form of expression and communication. The western world became more fully aware of the importance of movement and the way became open for movement, as a concept, to develop.

Normal movement happens spontaneously, quickly, fleetingly – and is forgotten in the next moment. Through movement teaching, however, the children can be helped to a greater awareness of movement and to the factors that are inherent in movement expression . . .

1 Body awareness.
2 Body activity.
3 Relationship of self to space and other people.
4 Awareness of quality of movement.

Through a process which involves looking, feeling, sensing, copying, expressing, experiencing and projecting, the children are building up a wider resource of expression, through which they can express their inner feeling, mood and ideas. They are undergoing experiences that are not only concerned with movement itself, but which are part of the integrated process that is total education.

Expressive movement is therefore of prime importance for a variety of reasons. First of all, it allows the children direct, immediate, spontaneous expression of their intimate feelings. At the same time, it enables the children to derive pleasure and enjoyment from being able to express these feelings easily and freely. As skill in the control of the body is developed, this feeling of pleasure will be heightened and many children succeed in co-ordinating both mind, body and imagination in the production of an 'end product' which is vital and lively. This is important for all children but is especially so for those who might lack the ability to write creatively or to work with concrete material such as clay. Their own bodies are perhaps the only objects which these children can manipulate and shape easily. Through expressive movement they can enjoy the power of creation.

As the children cannot be fully creative without a vocabulary of movements they must learn through observation and awareness to collect a storehouse of remembered observed incidents. The teacher will use these to deepen the children's understanding of movement; so their own quality of moving will consequently develop and, in turn, will enhance the 'end product' that the children are creating. Their understanding of movement will go deeper than the superficial copying of aesthetic 'finishing' that perfects a ballet performance, for the children will not be concerned with the beauty of the image presented but rather with an awareness of strong and light actions, dominant and submissive ones, sudden and forceful actions, easy and awkward movements, flexible and sustained movements.

Expressive movement, however, needs some tightening control and this can be achieved with the aid of a partner. Learning to work with a partner or group will help to deepen the children's understanding of the relationship of the body to the outside world, and this will be further developed through learning skills with small apparatus. These are important as they help to train the children to observe, to judge distance, and to co-ordinate eye, muscle, limb and the whole body. The process of throwing an object helps the children to learn about speed, action and movement: the need to relate the position of the body to an object that is not really part of itself. Waving the hand up and down, can be developed into an action that involves patting an actual bouncing ball – the ball though separate from the body is at the same time almost an extension of the body. The sequence re-explored without the ball, allows the children to mime the action with deeper understanding and awareness of the activity. The development of the skills of motor co-operation through the co-ordination of mind and body make the children aware not only of the total body but of specific parts of the body. This helps them to know exactly what the different parts can do by themselves, or how one part can combine with another part to fulfil a different kind, or series, of actions. It is important that children should understand the different actions which separate parts of the body can perform. As they become more aware and learn the necessary skills and control of a well disciplined body, so confidence in self and the ability to utilise the body will grow. Likewise the more skilled they become, the more they will be able to enjoy joining in group games or movement exploration.

Agility on fixed apparatus will complete the process of body awareness. Here the children are presented with a totally different kind of problem. They have to learn to deal with the relationship of the body to a concrete unyielding object and they have to learn to discover the best means of manipulating themselves under these new conditions. The apparatus is in no way an extension of the body and it is totally alien. Because of the fixed nature of the object it is obvious that only certain movements will be possible and this limitation presents yet another problem. The children have to answer this problem conciously by organising the body in relation to the fixed object. Initiative is brought into the forefront of the movement process. The children themselves have to order the methods they will use to climb up or down. They will have to answer the problem before the action takes place: whereas the action in the other forms of movement are an almost unconscious reaction. The successful accomplishment of these somewhat more complex tasks will help the children to have even greater confidence in themselves. At the same time, the children are exercising various muscles which are not usually exercised in their normal daily movements. Thus we see that this kind of functional movement has a kind of therapeutic purpose.

Basically, all three forms of movement – physical education and games; normal physical challenges in everyday life; and expressive movement – are exercising the body and helping it to develop as a functional machine. This simple fact should not be overlooked when considering the other more complex factors such as stimulating awareness, developing manipulative skill and the stimulation of imagination. All three forms are equally important.

The ability to control and make the body respond as a unit is important, for it enables children to respond to a stimulus with a precise clarity of movement. If the children have been properly encouraged they react simply or dramatically. The response is no longer an uncontrolled emotion-motivated movement.

Children are concerned with the expression of an idea and will be able to draw upon their imagination to colour this response. They can add their own mouthed or percussion sounds using simple instruments to deepen the involvement, finally being able to explore self-invented phrases and dance sequences.

In this final stage, they will be intellectualising all that they have learnt, yet it is interesting to note that the educational process is not unlike the natural development of ceremonial dance in primitive society. This substantiates Ouspensky's beliefs that movement is concerned with the deepest human emotions and with the healthy development of both the individual and society. It cannot be left out of our educational structure.

What is creative drama?

Whereas movement is concerned with helping children to gain control and mastery over their own bodies, creative drama is concerned with helping the children to gain mastery over their intellectual and linguistic powers. It enables them to develop the ability to use words effectively and flexibly in ordinary conversation, simultaneously allowing them to express and affirm their perception of reality and the world around them.

Through a programme which includes participation in normal conversation, discussion, oral awareness, simple speech exercises and playlets, the children are gradually encouraged to speak freely.

Their repertoire of words is extended in the first instance during story time, but this depends on the children being both receptive and able to participate actively. Children do not automatically know how to listen properly and cannot concentrate for fairly long periods without losing interest and becoming bored. Therefore it is essential to select stories carefully so that the children look forward to story time and are willing to concentrate. At the same time they need to learn how to be a good audience. Some children brought together in a group, bring out the worst in each other; some quarrel, jostle for front seats, or seize an opportunity to pinch a supposed enemy. Others fidget or try to talk to a neighbour. What constitutes a good audience? It is certainly not rows of children sitting stoney faced and subdued, seemingly afraid to show their feelings. Rather it is an audience which though sitting quietly is listening carefully, fully aware and thoroughly appreciative. Enjoying the humour, laughing at the comical incidents or feeling moved and sympathetic in the sad parts. Identifying with characters, ready to join in if asked to do so. A good audience is therefore children consciously concentrating on something which interests them.

It is better if the children sit on the floor around the teacher, for a feeling of intimacy grows more readily in this type of situation. If the teacher acts out the tale with gestures and facial expressions, then the children will become used to gestural statements as a means of unfolding a tale. If the story permits, the children should be encouraged to join in with finger play actions, or mouthed sounds so that they are not merely listening but taking an active part in the story. Here they are being introduced to the value of sound effects as a means of heightening a theme in drama. Audience participation, whenever possible, adds to the children's enjoyment and helps to increase their ability to listen.

Just as story time extends the children's vocabulary, so free play in the Wendy House allows them to use these words in ordinary play conversation. Nothing is imposed on them, instead they are required to be entirely in command of the exploration, to invent the story, the words and the actions naturally for themselves.

Wendy House drama in fact is probably the best method of entering and exploring creative improvised drama. One has only to watch children during free play Wendy House activities; they are completely absorbed; unconcerned with children outside the play situation, even unaware that they themselves might be being observed. Often the playlet, in which they are involved, is a work-out of a real life incident which they have witnessed, and the theme is plastic enough to permit other children to join in or to leave the activity in much the same way that people visit or leave an ordinary household. During the play the children act out quite naturally the character they are supposed to be: mother, father, dog. If the theme is more imaginative, perhaps based on cowboys and Indians, the children become deeply involved. If the need arises for movement and travel, the boy playing the part of the cowboy will pretend to leap on to a horse, then will change into the dual role of being both horse and rider rolled into one. He will command the horse to stop and will then neigh and buck and rear during the process of stopping. Indeed, one six year old boy, engaged in exploring a cowboy theme changed from being simply the cowboy, to being horse, then rider who fell mortally wounded. Suddenly he resurrected himself in the guise of a mysterious stranger who had come to save the situation. During this part of the exploration he jumped up and down repeatedly, changing quickly from being a stranger to being the cowboy, and back again, speaking for both in turn until finally the cowboy died and the stranger rode back to the fort to tell his friends of his death. Speech and movement come freely at such a time. Yet the same child would become tongue-tied if asked to come and speak in front of the class. Consequently it is necessary to allow the children to explore these free plays frequently and to back up this with plenty of involvement in other forms of language work until they become confident in their own ability and can feel happy to act with other children in front of other children.

Through controlled improvisations stemming from these first explorations in the Wendy House, the child is able to find himself, to discover his personality, his potentialities and limitations, his movement and language capacities and his particular interests. He is enabled and helped to understand himself as a total person, emotionally, physically and intellectually. He is able to become more confident in himself and to develop confidence in his immediate abilities and is encouraged to strive to improve them. He is able to become more aware of other people and to develop a sensitivity towards them. In this sympathetic climate he is allowed to 'open up' and reveal a side of his character which might not otherwise be revealed to the world at large. Each exploration aids this opening-up process and helps the child to give and say a little more than in his previous improvisation. It helps him to crystallise his own impressions about life and it encourages him to work out solutions to his worries and problems in a form that is somewhat therapeutic and which he is able to understand.

Early involvement in frequent drama activities is therefore essential in a child's education, for the sooner he develops the ability to control his emotions, actions and thoughts and learns to verbalise and communicate his ideas spontaneously, quickly and adequately, the sooner he is being equipped with a valuable aid and tool in life – a form of triple confidence: verbal, social and physical/emotional controlled confidence, without which a person cannot project himself to other

1 *Free activity in the Wendy House*

people as a fully integrated adequate person. This is emphasised only too clearly in the following school report of an American schoolgirl (quoted in a newspaper on 5 August 1969):

> 'She has a failure to conceptualise and an inability to verbalise sufficiently which is causing her grave self doubts. Her lack of confidence causes neuroses, impedes her capability to communicate with her peers.'

If a child is to feel secure in himself as a person, it is necessary that he is allowed to develop complete awareness of the extent of his physical and emotional ranges together with the knowledge that he can control and learn to discipline these so that he can act sensibly and speak with sensibility.

Without the understanding that he can control most of his actions and vocabulary he is unsure, frightened and liable to be rather unstable when faced with a novel situation. It is essential, therefore, to integrate activities often with other subjects so that the child is progressively helped to develop a completely integrated knowledge of himself as soon as possible, together with confidence in his own various activities so that he can fit easily and happily into a working group and integrate more fully into social life, both at school and at home.

At the same time, home and school are brought closer together as the child explores incidents observed at home during work in school. In turn, the improvisations enable the child to see how activities in school can link up with the outside world. The improvisations help to inter-relate and deepen the child's understanding of the world.

Children need plenty of time, however, to find out about themselves and the world, they do not perceive as adults do, but only perceive what is pertinent to themselves at a particular time or stage in their physical or imaginative development, eg two quite intelligent boys (friends) stated that they had been to London together with their parents, and during the visit had seen the Queen drive past in her car. Both children said she had been wearing a blue dress, yet one, the factually minded boy said she had worn a dark hat. The other, (highly artistic and imaginative) said she had worn dark hair and a glittering beautiful crown. (Perhaps, therefore, they had 'seen' what they needed to see!)

Similarly, children's drawings often allow us to see how they view the world, eg a five year old's drawing of the school playground clearly show us how he sees, feels and fears it.

2 *A child's drawing reveals his fear of the playground*

In the original drawing there is a curious picture of loneliness, of waiting and watching, of personal isolation. The teacher on playground duty is a large watchful head, without body, because 'she was moving about all the time'. The child himself had a textured jersey, trousers and firm legs, but hardly any head . . . 'Because', he said, 'I do not know what I look like'. Two children stand nearby, curiously their hands are pinchers. (Oddly enough the boy is very unhappy and often in tears because other children have hurt him, usually by pinching him.) The other children are somewhat nebulous people, perhaps because he rarely plays with them or joins in group activities for work. It is a sad comment about the inherent loneliness of maladjusted, withdrawn children and it emphasises the need to help them to try to integrate into social life. Drama and movement can often help to begin this process of integration. Certainly, it provides the easiest and most useful starting point, provided the child feels the teacher at least is his friend.

It is, however, necessary that the children should be allowed to gain this confidence and understanding at their own speed. To attempt to force its development could be harmful, if not actually damaging, to a sensitive child. Therefore if drama activities are to be of value in the child's natural development process, great patience is needed, for the process is slow and lasts throughout school life. Each involvement in movement and drama activities should be regarded not so much as a complete specific lesson, but rather as part of a total process.

The immediate improvisation or exploration, though apparently complete in the statements which are arrived at, and apparently concluded during the actual lesson, is still only part of a complex series which continues to develop during the whole period that the child is in school. Week by week this seems to have little immediate relevance to the overall development process of the individual child but over the entire programme provides him with the opportunity to develop a better understanding of himself and of other people . . . (how they might react in certain circumstances and how he himself might behave). He learns gradually through active personal involvement something about himself, he is led to discover his interests, his potentialities and his limitations, in fact he is helped to be proud to show and to project himself to other people.

The young child is not consciously aware of this process of self discovery. He still cannot make judgments or assessments on the same level that adults do, but he can be helped towards making the basic discoveries that begin the process through a series of events which combine into finding out; thinking about, and commenting on.

The child believes he is enjoying himself and just participating, it is the teacher who must be fully aware of the actual progress of each individual child, and be ready to help him by allowing him plenty of time to observe, comment, adapt, adopt, discover, assimilate, try out, and project his new ideas and discoveries (always helping him to build on to already absorbed knowledge). Obviously it is necessary to arrange the process of improvised involvements so that the themes will both allow the child to use his native gifts and at the same time develop his true linguistic powers as he widens his vocabulary, and develops the ability to make and use a clear cut phrase.

Themes can be re-explored many times, for a child's experience is transitional and he can benefit from the re-investigations, through his wider range of experience. At the same time spontaneous improvisations provide an easy method of enlivening and linking most subjects in the primary school lessons, and subjects come alive as the children discover and remember essential facts during the enjoyable process of acting out and re-telling the basic facts. And a higher appreciation and interest in the subject follows the dramatization. Quite often the immediacy of the situation, the urgency to communicate, the freedom from on-stage-level acting, and the lack of heavy stultifying props, stimulates many children with a keen desire to participate and they become eager to volunteer to take part in the free improvised playlets, mimes or expressive movements and dance interpretations. Some of the themes form an important link with out of school activities, others link up with different classroom activities and so permit the child to fit together and utilise knowledge discovered during other subject research, or through personal involvement in 'centres of interest', in a way that makes sense to the child. During the process of working out a basic idea that may arise out of movement or verbal based drama stimulus, activities can bridge subjects, ie the child can work quietly in the art corner, exploring both his imagination and art skills as he fashions himself a mask which he might later use in movement, mime or verbal drama explorations.

Naturally, the older and more able children can work at a deeper and more rewarding level, but even infants can utilise linked activities during the process of working out a basic idea that grows during movement or verbal drama explorations. For example, a group of six year olds (who had already had considerable experience in both basic verbal and movement activities) became interested in exploring the theme about robots. A child had casually mentioned to the teacher that he had seen a film on television in which creatures from space were present. Several children had seen this film and immediately an animated discussion arose about space, space creatures, robots, daleks, etc. The children spontaneously began to imitate the somewhat stilted arm movements of the robots and to move about in a stiff kind of way. Another child suggested that a simple play might take place. This was permitted but it soon became evident that the children were not satisfied with their first attempts. During the follow-up discussion they asked if they might have some cardboard boxes and rolls of corrugated cardboard to wear during the re-investigation of the idea. These were made available together with string, stapling equipment and painting material, scissors, measuring stick, etc. The children were allowed to get on with it, and the following group of photographs was taken during the morning's involvement.

3-6 Robots. Idea inspired by television programme

3 *Making robots*

4 *All dressed for action*

5 *Discovering the robot's limitations*
6 *A losing struggle to regain his feet*

Children who were not actively participating in the theme were not involved, and the play was not shown to the remainder of the class. Those who were taking part eventually dressed themselves in the painted costumes and worked out their improvisations, which included a battle. It was interesting to find that the children discovered, to their own amusement, that this particular type of stiff costume greatly hampered their movement possibilities. They also discovered how helpless they became if they were knocked over or fell down and that it was impossible to get on to their feet again without help from the so-called human inventor.

It led one child to remark that he had seen his toy robot at home kicking his legs in the air when it had fallen down and he had thought it funny. Now he knew how helpless the robot had actually been. He became extremely interested in discovering for himself how his own body movements became hampered under various conditions and he spent the whole of the afternoon making further personal explorations. He climbed into boxes of various sizes and compared the type of movements possible within the spacial area of the box. He explored running freely and running with his feet inside boxes and different shaped bags, he explored moving with his feet free and then tied together. He discovered how to arrange the weight of his body and to balance or unbalance and overturn the box. No doubt he might have made similar such explorations at some later date, but for this particular child at this particular moment the drama improvisation had provided the vital spark for a piece of intensive personal research.

It was evident that the whole group had enjoyed the social experience of working closely together as a team helping, advising and aiding each other. The work had been interesting because it encompassed number, art, movement, and speech in a meaningful way, and during the process the children had also experimented with finding the best method of fixing and holding the cardboard costume. The exploration had been satisfying and productive and enjoyable and led to two other projects, one concerned with machines which help man, such as tractors, and people who help man.

This example serves to illustrate the way in which drama is integrated into the daily work of the school. Yet at the same time the play being an extension of the child's world.

2 Teacher and child

The rôle of the teacher

The part which the teacher plays in the process of child development through creative movement and drama is very important. It is essential that she firmly believes that the learning process cannot be forced through an implanting of technique but can only be nurtured through a widening of the children's experience; as Dewey contends in *The Child and the Curriculum:* 'Moreover subject matter never can be got into a child from without. Learning is active. It involves reaching out of the mind. It involves assimilation from within. . . . Learning begins from within. Active involvement and participation not external imposition . . . it is freeing the life process for its own adequate fulfilment.'

It will be necessary for the teacher to build up a sympathetic atmosphere and establish a good rapport between herself and the children, for she will need to know each child extremely well. She must be prepared to interest herself in their 'little lives' so that she is both working in tune with them and is also tuned in to them, so that each child feels she is a good friend who likes and approves of him and who in turn is someone of whom the child can approve.

As A. S. Neil pointed out in *The Problem Teacher* . . . 'A good teacher does not draw out he gives out and what he gives is love. And by love I mean approval, if you like, friendliness, good nature. The good teacher not only understands the child, he approves of the child.'

Complete mutual approval and sincere honesty between teacher and children is the keystone and base on which the work must rest if the children are to benefit from involvement in drama activities. It is essential that the children believe that the teacher is a sympathetic person on whom they can rely, and that they do not feel she is critical of them or their performance or is bored by their effort. Otherwise they cannot make a true investigation, an honest statement or participate with real enthusiasm. The children must feel completely secure in the belief that the teacher is an understanding person who will respect them and their confidences, whether they are verbal comments or mime statements or movement responses, and that she is a person who is working with them as they strive to find the answers to their immediate problems.

It is important that the teacher realises that both the basic discovery work and the improvisations are only a means to an end and are not an end in themselves. Improvisations are not meant to be great art, neither are they a method of implanting a handed on technique of acting and dancing. They are simply an enjoyable means wherein the child can juxtapose his thoughts, ideas, observations and feelings and utilise his skills and knowledge to explore and interpretate his ideas.

Great care must be taken to be sure that the children feel they are free to join in, or not to join in the work, through individual choice. The work must be made to seem tempting so that they are lured into wanting to voluntarily participate. They must never feel that they are forced to involve themselves for that would drive the children away from this kind of creative work and might even make them dislike drama work of any kind. Consequently, the programme must be a free one. Some days there may be no improvisations, some days there may be several. At other times the children may pursue personal awareness discovery. Similarly children must feel that they are free to work individually with the teacher. Indeed some children are not ready to make class or group explorations and need time to find their own way into creative improvisations; eg a five year old became interested in mime work of a specific kind (developed out of a keen interest in observing everyday incidents). On several occasions he 'buttonholed' the teacher immediately before morning school, to show her his interpretation of some incident he had seen . . . One morning he plucked an imaginary rose from a tree, carefully wrapped the flower in silver paper and pulled it through his buttonhole and sniffed. The teacher was a little unsure of what the mime exactly represented. Seeing her hesitation the child said 'Oh dear' 'Can I try again?'

The second time he repeated his actions rather more slowly with more precision of movement and applying rather more thought to the effort. A successful guess from the teacher was rewarded with a beaming smile. Yet almost four months were to elapse before the child felt confident enough to join in a group exploration, although his subsequent progress was rapid and he was then able to direct and take part in several mime and verbal group explorations. Although these individual mime explorations were sometimes inconvenient, in the end the reward for both teacher and child was enormous.

Encouragement, patience and approval are essential qualities needed by the teacher. The teacher must therefore be willing to arrange her timetable to suit the children's needs. (An integrated day structure is perhaps the most suitable method, if it can be arranged to fit in with the framework of the school organisation.) At the same time the teacher must know very clearly in her own mind what particular aspect she is aiming for. How she is going to lead the children to learn to utilise sensory and body awareness in a creative way. Perhaps she might use teacher time in the classroom to engage the whole class in a very simple link up of exercises concerned with the hand awareness. She may channel the investigation to explore:

(a) an abstract response: that is opening and closing the hand quickly in response to a changing percussion rhythm
(b) an observed response: the abrupt movement associated with pricking the finger
(c) a response to literature: a series of hand movements suggested by the opening and closing of a flower described in a movement poem.

This responsibility in choosing avenues of development and the ways in which the choices are made, necessitates the examination of the four specific roles the teacher has to pursue.

1 LEADER

(a) Who instigates a sympathetic atmosphere and engenders confidence in the children, so that they are able to undergo and explore a piece of vital personal experience, during activities which require continuous listening, looking, feeling, as well as doing.
(b) Who leads through direct and indirect supervision. She may allow the children to work freely, sometimes without apparent close supervision, yet she always knows what is going on. She is constantly on the look out to ensure that all the children involved in an activity are actually gaining and benefiting from the involvement.
(c) Who understands the children sufficiently well to know which children will profit from working with close teacher supervision, or who will profit from working on their own, and those who will gain by joining in group work.
(d) Who knows when the children will benefit from working in linked basic activities rather than pure improvisation, and who senses when they are ready to move into improvisations.
(e) Who knows when to stretch through sympathy or praise, when to lead by a hint, discussion or concrete suggestion. No improvisation can be of the slightest use without guidance, direct or indirect from the teacher.

2 CONDUCTOR DIRECTOR

Who helps the children to make their own personal discoveries and helps them to collate and juxtapose these discoveries against those of their friends and other people so that they eventually form into a complex working whole.

At first the teacher will need to act as the main conductor director to whom the children look for guidance, watching for signals devised by herself, and previously explained to the children . . .

A non-verbal code (hand signals, raised eyebrows, nods, mouthed or percussive sounds) which permits the improvisations or investigations to develop without obvious interruptions, and which allows the children to move into or out of the involvement (either movement or verbal drama) in much the same way that the orchestra conductor can bring in or suppress the different various instruments during an exploration of a musical suite.

As soon as the children have some basic understanding of the use of signals the teacher should let all the children try their hand at being the Conductor during both mime and creative dance work. The aim being that the children can eventually explore both simple and complex investigations following directions given by their chosen child conductor/director.

This challenge is especially useful because sometimes a child is unable to join in a movement activity involvement or verbal drama exploration because he has a physical disability. (He may be deaf and dumb – or have 'rubber skin' which splits easily and needs to be stitched if he falls.) Working as a group director he is able to make quite a valuable contribution to the movement or verbal exploration, although he himself does not actually move about.

3 CONSULTANT

Who helps the children to find the answers to their problems, not through telling them 'how' or 'why' but through answering their questions with another question so designed that they are led to find the answer to their original query themselves. She must never allow herself to become a dictator imposing her conceptions of a response or character onto the children. She must always resist the temptation to show the children how to mime or act or put words into their mouths, for this would only be a stultifying procedure and would certainly not be a creative one. The children would only become conditioned and assume that they had been given a formula which would serve for all time . . . 'Miss says you act an old woman like so'! Henceforth the children would merely reproduce what they had been shown and would not bother to think for themselves. Further educational growth through creative drama activities would be impossible.

She must also lead the children to precede their investigation with a discussion and lead them to see the value of the discussions. Firstly, as a source of collation of ideas and inspiration, and secondly, as a kind of appraisal of work which provides a base on which to build further work. Although it may seem to be beyond the understanding of some of the younger children it is important to establish this process of discussion – investigation – discussion from the start for it establishes the idea of a sensible approach to the work, which will become part and parcel of the children's normal expectancy of drama involvement.

Without these discussions between teacher and children, the explorations become little more than an extension of playtime. Also during the discussions the teacher discovers something about the children's inner thoughts or development of logic. How they would possibly apply themselves to answer a problem, eg asked how she would cope with being lost and tired after a day trip in the country, a young child said, 'I would sit down on the grass and just wait for a tortoise to walk past. Then I would climb on his back and ride home'.

4 ARBITRATOR

Who helps the children to learn to be more sociable and able to work together in group activities. She is the person who sorts out temper tantrums which can arise during discussions or workouts either before, during or after the immediate dance or verbal drama involvement. Children often become angry and temperamental for the oddest reasons. A young girl was making her individual investigation during a verbal exploration (without props). She was fastening an imaginary cardigan when a boy observer suddenly shouted, 'You didn't fasten the last button'. A quarrel arose, because the girl insisted she had fastened all the buttons. The teacher was approached over the question. She asked the boy why he thought the last button had not been fastened. He said 'Because I counted and she fastened four buttons and there are five buttonholes'. Immediately the girl shouted, 'There may be five buttonholes but there are only four buttons because one came off and my mother was too tired and lazy to sew it on again'. (An interesting explanation considering the cardigan was an imaginary one!)

The boy accepted this explanation and the investigation continued without further interruption. It shows, however, the depth of involvement which the children find in these explorations.

Comments, audience involvement and sometimes audience participation during verbal workouts are part of the value of spontaneous improvised work.

The situation should always be free enough to allow for this, and permit a child to join in or leave an exploration if he has no more to say or is tired. The value of improvised work is that it is a form of involvement which is growing, changing and evolving throughout the duration of the particular exploration. Often a group of children may explore an idea and arrive at a conclusion and then decide to show their play to other interested children. It is not unusual for the play to begin in the same way but alter during the re-investigation. One group of six year olds in fact, worked out their play, showed it to the remainder of their class and asked if they might show it to a younger group. The teacher agreed that they could, provided that the other class found it was a convenient time to listen. Later she was interested to discover that the ending of the play had changed from being an unhappy one to being a happy one.

No doubt some children will develop an interest in one particular aspect of the work. Similarly, many teachers may emphasise one aspect more than another because of their own particular interests.

Some teachers may be Nature specialists, they may use the creative involvements mainly to deepen children's awareness of nature. While Art specialists may find that the art work is deepened through using movement as a stimulus prior to involvement in art work. Thus the children who are exploring a theme – perhaps concerned with Bonfire Night – might begin work by exploring some aspects of fire through movement. They might begin by lying down on the floor, curling in a ballshape. Then kick out legs and arms to suggest flames licking around wood. They might make small upward stretches of the body to suggest flames flaring up – these stretchings can increase to leaping and jumping as fire gathers momentum, until the whole body is exploring, leaping, jumping, rocking, swaying – as flames rise and fall. They might use flicking movements of fingers and hands to emphasise crackling and sparks flying. Thus the imagination will have been stimulated before they try to put their statement down in paint.

The teacher may therefore use movement as a stimulus from which to start work just as she may use a stimulus to spark off a movement response. She will need to find her own method of interesting the children in creative work and developing their powers of self-creative expression.

Children's ability

All children differ in ways and rates of learning and although most teachers are aware of this they often fail to understand why many children do not seem to progress in creative drama or movement. Often this is because they fail to realise that the main difficulty lies in the fact that some children are movement-shy, others word-shy – some are socially shy.

The socially shy child cannot respond because he is afraid that he may look silly or awkward in front of other children. He may be so shy that he cannot bear to enter a room full of people. He needs sympathetic encouragement so that he can overcome this difficulty. Even then he may continue to creep in quietly, sit near the door and engage himself in some quiet occupation which does not require him to be involved with other people: perhaps playing with a jigsaw, counting and sorting things, looking at books, reading, if he is able to do so. He may not be studiously inclined. He is concerned only with not drawing attention to himself. He needs to be coaxed to join in sense awareness and body awareness activities – so that he becomes used to focusing attention on himself and on other people. He needs to learn to relax. So activities which require him to unbend, eg slapping his arms across his chest and yelling are essential as they allow the child to overcome tension and inhibitions naturally, during the pleasure of making a simple group response. Everyone is busy slapping and yelling – so he cannot be making a fool of himself.

Often a child's ability to gain from creative involvement in drama depends on the degree to which he is able to relax and overcome nervous tension and shyness. Without complete relaxation, tensions build up and the children are hampered and bound by already acquired inhibitions and are hamstrung by their inability to unbend and 'let go'. Consequently it is necessary to help children to relax, for the ability to relax is an acquired art and is one that is of prime importance in creative work. The child who is completely relaxed is receptive and sensitive to new ideas and sensations and is aware of internal and external feelings. His mind is active, his body loose, his muscles slack, his vocal chords free. He is able to respond and work properly and consciously, and is able and ready to gain from his investigations because he is mentally, physically and emotionally, consciously aware of his immediate feelings and sensations. At the same time, he is completely aurally conscious of his present environment. Therefore he is totally receptive to the immediate experience and the experience is real and meaningful because it is spontaneous.

It is necessary, therefore, to include some exercises concerned with relaxation in the basic body awareness activities. At the same time, participation in basic awareness enables him to join in activities on an equal footing with other children, during which time he may begin to increase his vocabulary.

Many children have difficulty with creative drama work because they have an inadequate vocabulary. This may be conditioned by their home background – the language they hear and use at home.

It is quite adequate for a child's verbal needs when he is at home but is obviously limited when he is required to work with a more word-fluent child. He cannot follow the point of the conversation because he does not understand the words. Consequently he becomes inhibited unless he is allowed to develop his vocabulary. He must be encouraged to join in activities concerned with the use of language eg participation in storytime, especially poetry and movement work where he hears new words but is only required to respond through movement. At the same time he is able to hear how words fit to-together. Indeed, I have come across several children who spoke in monosyllables – milk, toilet, brick! They simply had not learnt to fit their words together to make up a phrase, let alone a sentence. So that a considerable amount of time was needed to persuade them to ask for their needs in sentence form 'May I go to the milk bar?', before work could begin on verbal drama.

A child may have a physical disability which prevents him from joining in activities which require physical participation and he is forced to sit on the side and watch, though it is evident he longs to join in. Often he is able to do so if the teacher allows him to become a group signals director. He can sit to one side of the room, yet is participating actively and is making a valuable contribution to the work.

Sometimes physical disability is verbally conditioned. He may be deaf, dumb or pehaps an immigrant, with little or no vocabulary. He is shy because he has difficulty in communicating his ideas and feelings to others, consequently he keeps his thoughts to himself. Often he has things to say which could make a valuable contribution to the lesson. He needs to be coaxed alone, slowly and praised for his efforts in mime and movement work which do not require speech. He can express his feelings easily and as he grows in confidence through his success in movement work so he will be encouraged to explore verbal drama. Often these children are able to move into fairly complex mime explorations within a short time because their daily life is rich and full and they have a store of remembered observations on which to draw. Many children possess an adequate vocabulary yet have a very narrow life which limits their ability to join in either drama or mime. Sometimes children from a cultured intellectual background may be hindered in their physical creative ability if they have been only the passive recipients of handed-on culture, especially if they have not been encouraged to supplement this knowledge with further discoveries of their own, or have not been required to think for themselves or engage in any form of self creative explorations. Often these children need a great deal of preliminary involvement in basic discovery activities before they can be helped to begin to work in a more creative way.

Many adults believe that children have an innate ability to respond to music. They believe that music will stimulate children emotionally so that they will naturally progress to make a physical response conditioned by the rhythm and pulse of the music. This is not strictly true. Some children may respond – many will not. Indeed some children are extremely movement-shy apart from being socially shy and need a great deal of encouragement and coaxing before they will join in expressive movement activities. These children are often happiest and progress quicker if they find their impetus through basic awareness activities. Nevertheless, some quite young infants who come from a sympathetic and enquiring home often possess the ability to utilise an open and reasoning mind which is already sharpened by imagination. They are therefore able to understand, participate and move into simple creative dance explorations without a great deal of involvement in basic awareness activities in school. They will still benefit by joining in the basic body, sensory, sound awareness with the class, but will be able to use this knowledge more quickly in a consciously creative way while their friends are still discovering the basic information and are struggling to find a way to use it. Equally the more mature reception class infant will be able to become involved in simple verbal drama explorations because they already possess an adequate vocabulary and are able to use it skilfully and confidently.

The starting point will therefore differ for each child. So the teacher must discover for herself those children who will eventually benefit most through creative movement explorations and those who will gain more by pursuing verbal improvised work. It is this, together with her own particular interest in either creative drama or expressive movement, which will probably determine the method which she finally chooses as the point of entry for the work involvement.

Personally, I have found that because some children are movement-shy, others word-shy and some who are skilful in both of these facts yet are socially shy, it is often necessary to find a common starting base. Consequently, in order to combat all these difficulties and in order to help the children feel that they are all starting together on an equal footing, it is often easiest, and useful, if the teacher introduces the children to the idea of compiling a 'personal dictionary' of common basic knowledge, based on awareness – a real awareness of self, sensations, sounds, vocabulary, movement and actions, locomotion and observations which will provide a basis and pertinent entry point for all future creative explorations (both movement and verbal) and which will allow all the children of varying abilities to begin to work happily together.

It is a simple personal dictionary which the children are led to discover and compile for themselves, including, for example:

1 Personal self awareness of body and awareness of body activity.
2 Awareness of sensations caused by feel of fur and velvets, etc. Smell and sound of bacon frying. Taste of salt and vinegar.
3 Awareness of movement.
4 Awareness of shape. Natural movements of wild life. Shape and texture of leaves.
5 Awareness of sounds made by bird trilling, trumpet, aeroplane. Noise of blown leaf. Rustling paper.

These are all different kinds of incidents which make a vivid impression momentarily on the mind at the time of occurrence and observation, which can be forgotten if the children are not encouraged to realise that they are not only worth noting but are also worth remembering. These basic discoveries provide the children with a functional working base which is necessary in exactly the same way that they establish a base leading to creative writing. The children develop an understanding of the mechanics of writing and learn to read and find words before they attempt to formulate and actively write down an original creative sentence. Just as the children are led to be able to think creatively in order to write creatively, so it is necessary to help them to think creatively before they can move and act in a creative way.

Few children possess the ability to think creatively and imaginatively in the abstract. Most children need to be able to conjure up a vivid mental picture from which to work, or on which to deepen a simple response into a simple phrase and sequence. Children need therefore to link up their basic awareness explorations as soon as possible and to try to turn them into simple expressive explorations. Even a young child can learn how to use a simple discovery about nature as a base on which to make a creative investigation. He can be asked to watch the clouds drift by in the sky, or observe water in the river nearby the school (as it laps on the bank or glides peacefully before gathering momentum, swirling around before it drops down to the dam or weir). He can be asked to try to express in simple actions and movement, something of the nature of the locomotive quality of the water (rolling his body along swiftly and slowly, rocking, twirling round, rising and sinking and jumping). He might explore the movements separately as he recalls and considers different parts of the stream separately – or he might fit them together into a movement sequence or dance. Similarly, the child can be encouraged to look at a plant, a succulent for example. He can be asked to note its size, general shape, colour. To feel it, to discover if it is hard, soft, rough, smooth, prickly, squashy, spiky, etc. He can be asked to talk about the plant and discuss what he sees and feels about its texture and shape, etc. He is making a straightforward discovery. Then he can be asked to look again at the succulent and to note something about the way the buds or leaves fit on to the stem. He can be asked to look at his fingers to see how they join onto his hand. He can be asked to use his fingers to express something of the spiky quality of the succulent leaves.

7 *A visual stimulus inducing a creative response*

He is beginning to juxtapose basic observation with a creative movement response exploration. Next he can be asked to consider the total shape of the plant, its twistedness or spreading out qualities, then to explore what kind of twistedness his own body is capable of making. This awareness can be deepened as he is asked to recall what he has observed about the plant's growth from the time it was planted to its present stage and he can be asked to explore a movement theme concerned with the plant's growth. This will probably entail curling up into a ball (as is a small seed), slowly opening out and growing upwards, twisting as he grows (if the plant he is recalling was twisted) until he reaches a final shape and utilises his fingers to express perhaps the final spikiness of the mature plant. Thus the child has been gradually led to turn a basic observation into a creative statement. At the same time he has become more fully aware of the actual growth of plants, and he has also made some progress in verbal work through his discussion about the succulent in the initial stages of the basic discovery. He has purposefully used some of the elements of movement, elevation, opening, closing, twisting, rising – space relationship and effort. Later, during a movement lesson in the hall, during a free response to sound stimuli, which is allied to an exploration of the theme growth, the child may be stimulated to move and make a more meaningful response to the activity, as he recalls his recent involvement in the classroom. It must be emphasised that the child is not asked to 'be' the plant, he is asked to express something of the nature and quality of the plant's movements during growth – pushing through soil, growing upwards, spreading outwards, growing twisted, stretching out in sunshine, closing at nightfall – shrinking and retreating into itself when withering and dying.

This kind of impetus to creativity and self expression is not limiting, for the child is consciously developing on from something he has seen, felt, explored, and which has been of immediate concern to him, however momentarily. He has been successful because the task has not been too difficult, for he has been asked to work from the level of immediate reality and has not been asked to make an imposed abstract mental effort or work in abstract vacuum. Rather, during the controlled involvement process he has been led through several linked stages to pass from straightforward discovery to make a creative and expressive statement about his basic discovery.

Quite often some children are thrown into a situation in which they are required to act a part in a school play or mime movement drama. Often they sink or swim according to their imaginative ability to assimilate teacher imposed acting formulae. No-one will deny that it is possible to involve children in this kind of drama work, and that results may seem to be achieved, but it is at best a superficial method and can have little real value in the full development of the children's true capabilites. Unless the investigation is allowed to develop from the children in a natural uninfluenced flow it can have little educative value and small effect on their personality or development of real confidence in themselves or their abilities.

Consequently, although the teacher must take care not to directly influence the children's creative responses, it is often necessary to help them to learn to structure and relate their discoveries so that they approach the problem of creative self-expression sensibly. Few children automatically know how to link up their immediate observations or response to stimuli with body awareness and sound awareness. It is necessary to help them to learn how they may juxtapose some of this information so that they can use it to make an expressive response and invent a creative sequence from the total juxtaposition.

As Dewey noted in *The Child and the Curriculum,* 'Nothing can be developed from nothing . . . Development does not mean just getting something out of the mind . . . it is development of experience and into experience that is really wanted.'

3 Sensory awareness activities

The aim of sensory awareness activities is fivefold.

1 To increase the children's actual knowledge (through capturing their interest in the process of discovery): to enlarge their vocabulary through talking and explaining about the objects.
2 To help the children to learn to concentrate.
3 To help the children to become aware of their reactions to sensations and at the same time to develop their ability to be able to touch things without fear, eg fur or feathers.
4 To encourage the children to gather together freely, to work together, to talk to each other, to learn to co-operate (a factor essential for drama work).
5 To provide the children with subjects for mime interpretations or with something to talk about which can be included in verbal drama work or provide the story base.

The process is very closely interlinked and lasts throughout the time the children are in school. So although the awareness exercises are the first of the work chapters it does not mean that they are simply beginnings. They are part of a continuing process helping to deepen all the other activities.

The ability to stand and stare, to look and see is a dominant quality which all children possess. Indeed most children are naturally far more observant than we suppose. It is necessary therefore to seize on this natural trait and help them to develop it to its fullest extent. Too often in the rush of every day life, adults tend to forget that the body can communicate and observe information with all the senses; and were we to go suddenly blind and deaf we would be forced to rely entirely on our non visual/aural senses for information. Yet, too often, we have not developed these other senses to a high degree because we have learnt mainly to rely on our eyes and ears. It is important therefore to make sure that children are given the opportunity to develop complete sensory sensitivity awareness to a heightened degree.

Time to stand and stare, to examine and feel should be an acceptable spontaneous part of the daily timetable, a time when the children should be free to simply observe. The time is not wasted, for the process becomes one of total involvement during the investigation, and their mind and body are alive, stimulated, sensing, questioning and experiencing with complete momentary concentration. The immediate impact can be enormous and can be reinforced if the children are encouraged to discuss what they have just experienced. In turn, this can be further deepened if they are encouraged to make a different kind of statement about the experience, through mime or art (painting, junk collage, a three dimensional model or a print).

Through touch

As soon as possible the teacher should build up a collection of various objects of tactile interest which can be placed on a table in the classroom, around which the children can gather to experience some of their reactions to sensations caused by touch. The children should be encouraged to bring into class other objects which they think may be interesting and which can be added to the already assembled collection which should be constantly growing and changing as the children become more personally concerned with the work as their initial interest is developed.

The 'sensation' table should contain such things as empty textured boxes, fircones, leaves, stones, fibre boards, pieces of rubber, leather, string, pieces of glass, plain ribbed, textured (framed), jelly, sandpapers, hair, sheepswool, fibre glass, nylon, plastic, polystyrene, lino, corks, rope, textured papers, assorted bottles, pieces of material, satins, woollens, velvets, organdies, gauze and corrugated cardboard. The various objects should be unadulterated and preferably should *not* be mounted on small wooden blocks through the mistaken belief that children find these easier to handle or that they stack more easily. The wooden block in fact defeats the purpose of the sensation response, especially if the material mounted is, for example, corduroy or textured satin. Much of the sensation stimulus of the materials comes from their inherent softness and this is cancelled out by the hardness of the block underneath.

The children should feel the objects with their finger tips. Hold them in one hand, then enclose them in both hands to experience the total shape and weight of the object. They should also be encouraged to place the object against their neck, cheek or leg, so that they experience the object with whole body reaction and not only with fingers and hands. If the object is clean and suitable the children might place it against their lips and perhaps even on the tip of the tongue. They should be asked to close their eyes and feel it as a blind person must, and also to smell it.

The children should be allowed to tickle each other with feathers or cotton wool, to ascertain sense reactions on arms, legs, under chin, etc. They should also be encouraged to develop a feeling for quality in movement while they are exploring the tactile surfaces. For

8 *Sensory awareness: touch. Clive, Shirley and Fotoula feel the softness of fur and feathers*

9 *Sensory awareness: touch. Howard and Gary feel the springy quality of raffia bunched together*

instance, when they are stroking and feeling fur pieces, reference should be made to the fur on animals. They should be asked to pretend the fur is a pet kitten and, as such, stroke it slowly and gently, with sustained movements. This can be developed into a simple verbal drama exercise if they are encouraged to talk to the imaginary animal.

Suitable material from the sensation table could be used for making junk prints or collages with plaster or clay as soon as its immediate use as a 'sensation' is finished, it might be used to take a direct cast of a suitable object. In this way such things will not remain set apart from the sensation table but will become acceptable and familiar work materials.

At the same time, large pieces of fabrics should be made available, so that the child can experience the weight and quality of various materials as they sort them into collections concerned with colour, texture, length. While they are sorting, they might be persuaded to pretend they are sorting laundry which they will do quickly with darting rapid movements as they flick through the clothes. They can pretend to scrub and rub with circular strong, rhythmic movements. Next they can pretend to wring them and hang them out to dry, using swinging elevated arm and body movements. They might even be persuaded to explore the movements of washing, hanging, flapping and waving as the 'clothes' are dried by the wind.

The children should be allowed to drape the material around themselves, so that they can develop an understanding of the peculiar properties of various fabrics; how some drape and fold easily whilst others cannot be draped properly at all. They should be encouraged to utilise the lengths of materials to make spontaneous costumes which they can wear for fun, or use in an impromptu exploration, and at the same time discover how movement can be hampered by different skirt lengths: that, for instance, a long, full, flowing nylon skirt will make little difference to their striding habits (though they might trip over it at first) whilst a long tight woollen skirt will prevent long steps being taken and may even require the child to take mincing steps rather than only short ones. They may discover that a skirt of this type will hinder their ability to climb on a box or rostrum which perhaps represents a bus step. They may discover that they cannot sit or bend down if their costume is made from corrugated cardboard. They will see and discover that flimsy material will waft as they walk and rise and whirl around their hips as they twirl around; that heavier material will hang and drag around the ankles and will need to be gathered up and even held in their arms if they wish to climb a staircase. The children are thus discovering something about the influence which costume can have on an actor's movements. At the same time the activity might provide a link with the study of the history of costume.

Children appreciate seeing themselves in these costumes, so it is useful to have a looking glass. Not only do they see what the outfit looks like, but they can see which materials are transparent and which are not.

Children should be given some opportunity to explore different tactile surfaces underfoot. Every opportunity should be taken to allow them to stand and walk about on different surfaces – sand, gravel, stones, tarmac, grating, ribbed surfaces, ropes, textured papers, cloth, marble slabs – and to paddle in water. Their attention should be drawn to the actual sensation they are receiving from standing on these various surfaces. Is it hot, cold, prickly, does it feel safe, secure, rocky, do their feet sink into it, etc? They should also be asked to listen to the sound their feet make on the surfaces when they wear gym shoes, day shoes, or are barefooted. Something of the quality of footsteps should be noted. Children rarely pay attention to the quality of movement unless it is specifically pointed out.

The children should be encouraged to make a 'touch walk' in a safe area of the school. perhaps in a corner of the playground where they can safely walk about with their eyes shut, and ascertain exactly where they are by feeling the surface of the walls, door, trees, etc. that form the boundary of the area. If it is possible, older children should be taken on a touch walk investigation of an area nearby the school. They should be encouraged to notice, feel and perhaps take rubbings of the pattern of bricks, linked nettings, tarmac roads, coal hole covers, decorative gates, leaves, pavement cracks, trellis work, etc. This is important, for the children need to know the area between home and school really well, so that they can bring it to mind and form a vivid mental picture of it. Thus when they are interpretating a theme concerned with an old man crossing a road, they can recall a certain street near the school and imagine that the man is crossing this street, they will know when he might have difficulty hobbling across the cobblestones, where he might stride across a drain cover on to the pavement where his steps would be firmer and his gait steadier.

The teacher should also make up several sensation stimuli feel boxes. These may be large or small, but must be totally enclosed except for a sleeve entrance, which is long enough to provide access to the container, but which will not permit the children to see into the box even though they look down the sleeve. The sleeves may fit into the top, side or bottom of the box according to convenience. The teacher should glue, hang or place various single objects inside

10 *Sensory awareness: touch. Jane and Amanda feel the different textures of fabrics*

11 *Sensory awareness: touch. Angela, Sandra and Clive dive into the sense stimuli box*

each box, eg jelly, scrubbing brush, which the child must feel and experience by touch alone. It is necessary to inform the children before they place their hands in the sleeve opening that there is nothing in the box which will hurt them in any way. Thus without a feeling of fear, they can immediately react to the sensation of touching the unknown object. The sensation is heightened because the child must rely on his fingers and hands to convey the information to his brain. The children should be encouraged to talk about their sensation as they are still exploring the feel of the object. They should be asked to say what they think it might be. They may guess correctly, or they may possess a vivid imagination and invent a highly unlikely solution. (Two children's reactions to a scrubbing brush were a sleeping baby hedgehog, and a moustache which a giant has shaved off!)

Some children should be allowed to witness their friends make these feel investigations in the feel boxes. They should be asked to note their friends' movements and to observe their facial expressions. After the immediate feel investigation is over, a small group might try to mime something of what the investigator did and try to portray something of his facial response. In this way they are learning to appreciate something of the value of gesture and facial expression as important facets of mime.

Next the children might be introduced to feel stimuli parcels. The teacher should select various assorted objects of interesting size and shape and varying in tactile quality, eg rope, brass candlesticks, key, shredded wheat, plastic bottle, wooden toy. She should wrap these singly into odd shaped parcels which, to some extent, disguise the actual size of the object. Thus a small matchbox might be loosely wrapped in tissue paper so that it seems bigger than it actually is, and a brass object might be tightly wrapped in waxed paper so that the parcel seems small. Thus the children simultaneously discover that a large parcel is not always heavier than a small one; that size does not define actual weight. The children should be encouraged to hold and handle the parcel with both hands, to try to feel and trace the shape of the hidden object as they attempt to discover what the parcel contains. It should be passed along the group and then when all the children involved in the activity have felt it, they should begin to compile what each child thought he had felt and also their ideas as to what it might be. The parcel should then be opened and the object revealed. The children can see the object, feel it, and begin to discuss how it was made, what it is, what its real uses might be. They may be encouraged to make up a story about it, perhaps how it was lost, when, where, why (accidentally or on purpose), what had happened to it while it was lost, who has found it again and what will happen now. Thus the children are beginning to work out for themselves a theme and story which can be further explored during a mime or verbal exploration.

Through taste

Whenever possible the teacher should provide things which the children can taste or sip under controlled conditions; blackberries, crab apples, rhubarb, mustard and cress, carrots, pomegranate seeds, coconuts, dry grain bread, peas, pulses, licquorice root, milk, water, soda water, etc. The children should be encouraged to sip or chew very slowly so that they really do experience the process of chewing and tasting the food before it is finally swallowed. If the food is suitable, and if there is sufficient, a portion should be held in the hands, felt, sniffed and examined before a second portion is tasted and eaten.

12 *Sensory awareness: taste. Fotoula tastes dry bread*

Conscious eating and drinking under a controlled situation provides the children with a heightened awareness of the food and drink, and they receive an entirely different sensation from that which is normally experienced when food is eaten quickly.

They should be allowed to taste sugar, salt, pepper, vinegar, mustard, lemon, etc., in another controlled situation, and be encouraged to place a pinch on the tip of the tongue, to savour it, then to swallow it; to rinse the mouth before placing another pinch on the side or back of the tongue. In this way they become more aware of the different tastes of the various items and also discover the different taste buds in the tongue and so can realise that different parts of the tongue convey different taste information to the brain. Thus they can discover that the tongue can feel as well as taste. They should notice the difference of feeling experienced when the tongue touches a soft substance (butter) or a hard bone surface. It might be explained that the tongue is used to help us to swallow and so link the work with a biology lesson.

Similarly, they should be encouraged to explore the process of drinking, during an investigation of milk, water, fruit juices. They should be encouraged to sip the liquid slowly and consciously and, before swallowing, to roll it around the mouth and fully explore the taste and experience its warmth, or coldness on the lips, side of mouth, under the tongue, on roof of mouth, as well as on the tongue itself. Children generally do not bother to do this, but drink quickly merely to slake their thirst. Consequently they do not appreciate some of the elements or stages of drinking which can be explored in mime drama.

The children should be asked to watch their friends and family as they eat and drink under normal circumstances, to note if mother holds her cup by the handle with one hand, or if a friend holds her beaker between two hands with the fingers clasped around the glass feeling the warmth of the liquid. They should be encouraged to notice if the friend drinks the liquid completely in one go, or if mother sips slowly and thoughtfully, perhaps resting her elbow on the table as she holds a cup; or if father sips his tea, and replaces the cup on the saucer as he engages in conversation with mother. Whether he sits back afterwards and relaxes in his chair. These are all incidents which children can explore in mime and are ones which can add richness to an interpretation if the children have become aware of their value and existence.

Small cups, large beakers, straws and bottles should be available in the classroom so that some children who are interested may try out and investigate some of the actions they have observed people make, when they were engaged in eating and drinking. The children are concerned with exploring an actual happening or incident which they have witnessed. Consequently it is essential that they have props. Their approach is a scientific investigation, they are concerned with feeling the actual weight of the liquid in the cup as it is held in the hand (water is perfectly adequate for this purpose), and the children are quite content with a few cheese biscuits as well.

Without this kind of preliminary work a mime presentation is often shallow because the children are merely miming the action of picking up and putting down a cup. They forget that the weight of the liquid influences the way the cup is held, or that it can cause an accident, and the cup spills over as the wrist twists unexpectedly. They must notice the way the hand is used to actually pick things up.

It is very important that the teacher makes sure that the children understand that they must not taste or touch anything on the taste table if she is not in the room, and that they do not place any kind of food or drink on the table unless she has examined it and expressly given them permission to do so. She must also instruct them that they must not pick and eat berries or leaves as they walk home from school.

The children should also be encouraged to taste, using the tip of the tongue to feel and taste clean, splinter-free objects such as an unpeeled orange/apple, plastic cube, pine cone, or clean white paper in an extension of touch awareness activities.

Through smell

From time to time the teacher should introduce a smell shelf into the discovery corner of the classroom. The children should be encouraged to bring things from home which they like to sniff such as empty talcum powder boxes, face powder containers, bath salts, perfumed soap, scented wrapping papers, detergent containers, herbs and flowers. As a wise precaution they should be discouraged from bringing jars or tins which have contained medicants, in case a trace should still be left in the bottom of the tin and which might be harmful to taste or rub on their eyes. Likewise the children should be told they definitely must not bring old lipstick containers. These are rarely completely used up and the children use the remnants and mark their clothes in the process.

The objects should be placed on the shelf and the children can sniff to their hearts' content, and discuss the various scents.

The teacher can add to the collection by bringing empty spice jars, cocoa and coffee tins, freshly baked bread, fruits, mosses, grass cuttings, soil, peat and if the school is not overheated, fish and shell fish, cheese, onions and cat mint. Thus the children receive an all round assortment of odours and are not required only to sniff sweet scented perfumes. The children can discover the smell of chrysanthemums and be able to compare this with old-fashioned sweet scented roses. They should be made to understand that nothing can be placed on the smell shelf until it has been shown to the teacher and then only after she has given permission to place it there.

The smell table can also be a source of ample material to be explored in mime investigation as the children are called upon to watch their friends' facial expressions as they react to the different smells, and re-interpretate what they have seen in a mime exploration.

Discovery walks often form part of the class programme. Usually, the children are taken round the area surrounding the school and are generally required to notice things which will aid project work concerned with nature, history or environmental studies; perhaps industries in the area.

Sense stimulation is rarely the prime concern of discovery walks. Yet if it were, it could provide an interesting alternative and one which might stimulate the children to take a more active interest in the area. For example, the children could be taken on a walk concerned with discovering the number of different smells which are to be found in a given area. One group of children were in fact on such a walk. As they were reception class children, the walk was limited to a narrow alley which ran behind the school and was bounded by market gardens. It led to a small weir, from which a narrow path ran to the main road and a busy shopping centre. The smells which were encountered on the way included, flowers in the garden, mown grass, manure, and rotting vegetables in the market garden, damp earth by the river, pungent smell of onions frying in house. Various smells emanating from fish and chip shop, greengrocers, butchers, bakery, turpentine from wallpaper shop, and petrol from the garage on the main road, exhaust from traffic.

Through visual observation

The children should be helped to realise that careful visual observation can play a leading part in developing their awareness of the world and of people around them. The ability to concentrate and look deeply into or at an object can be fostered, if objects of interesting shape and colour are made available for inspection. These should include things which are obviously meant to capture the children's interest and persuade them to gather around the interest table;

colourful badges, beads, small toys, ships in bottles, bottles which have been malformed by heat, discarded film negatives, coloured celluloids and plastics. All these the child can use to change his immediate impressions of everyday things.

As soon as the children have noticed the interest table contents, other more educational objects should be added to the collection such as sawn-off twisted branches or tree roots, shells, fossils, fir cones, decorative plastic tiles, fibreboards, interesting shaped bones (and skeletons or skulls when available) half sections of fruit and vegetables decorative lace, scientific movement toys, zoetrope, kaleidoscope prism, some of which can be made by the children.

13 Sensory awareness: vision. Sandra examines a pineapple

Often it is possible to make a collection of microphotographs which show details of natural objects or sections of man-made objects, or photographs which present an object from an unusual angle. If these can be displayed on the wall immediately above the interest table, and the real or similar object be displayed on the table below, the children often become interested in comparing the object and the photograph, and in turn try to discover which part of the object the photographer had been interested in especially if a magnifying glass or small microscope is made available.

The children should be encouraged to make paintings, pattern and prints using either the actual object or information they have gathered as the starting point of the work. These in turn could form a second departure point for children who have some movement experience.

Infants can be coaxed into making a more intense inspection of an object which may not particularly appeal to them. They might have picked up a fir cone and put it down after a quick glance. It is possible to make them regard it more closely in a second inspection if they are asked to see if there are any spiders hiding under the bract, and it is possible to persuade them to talk about what they can see while they are looking. One child so engaged did not comment very much on the texture or tactile quality of the fir cone, but became extremely interested in the space between the bracts, and explored putting his fingers into the gaps. He talked for a long time afterwards about dark spaces, and black holes and night, and space travel, yet his drawings which were made later, showed that he had observed the plant in great detail although he had not talked about its shape or textured surface, at the time of the investigation.

The children should be asked to study their friends more closely. Perhaps they might choose one child who will be the subject for scrutiny by the group. She might stand, sit or engage herself in an activity such as reading. The group watch her for a few minutes, they can either draw the child while she is still present, or she can be sent away whilst the others engage in a verbal game in which they try to recall what she was wearing, what colour were her eyes, how did she hold the book? Often it is evident that children see only that which has emotional appeal to them. They will be able to describe in detail a brooch or the pattern of the child's jumper, yet will have no clear knowledge of the actual colour of her eyes though they have noticed the freckles above her cheek bones.

They should be encouraged to note any personal mannerism which may expose something of the character of personality of the person they are observing; nail biting, thumb sucking, hair twisting, ear rubbing, screwing up of bottom of dress, pulling trouser leg up and down, collar sucking, jumper biting, foot tapping. Once the children have become aware that the existence of such details may be important in the development of an interpretation of a character they become keen to keep a look out for them.

A class of five-year-olds were asked to describe their mothers waiting at the gate. They seemed bewildered and rather unsure what their mothers looked like. A second question was asked, 'If you look out of the window, how do you know which is your mother?' Three replies were, 'I look for a yellow hat and a pair of glasses.' 'She's the scruffiest mother there.' 'I know my mother because she's a pretty good shape.' But the children were unable to deepen these first descriptions. After a long discussion about people, types of clothing, ways of standing and nervous habits, etc, the children were asked to go home and 'really' look at mother so that the following day another attempt could be made at describing mother – or father or another adult who may have been interesting to observe.

Their descriptions the following day were somewhat more enlightening. One child said that 'her mother has real eyes but she sticks false ones on top and she wears clippers to hold up her stockings.' Without being asked, the child made a spontaneous attempt to mime her mother making up her face and struggling into a roll-on and fastening her stockings, stepping into a dress and pulling the zip up. Another child sat down and mimed winding an endless bandage around the right leg and then the left leg (his mother had varicose veins) yet he had not thought of mentioning the bandages the day before. A third child, rather shy, who rarely joined in verbal discussion, jumped up and pursed her lips, quickly stretched them into a wide grimace and pursed them quickly again. She repeated this several times, whereupon another child yelled 'That's not your mother, that's your auntie.' This simple mime depicting a nervous trait, had indeed adequately conveyed and depicted the aunt's facial nervous habits, and in fact had conveyed quite a strong mental image of the aunt to the other children, who immediately began to discuss the aunt, recalling other finicky habits which she had, as well as describing her clothes and hairstyle. Consequently, the exercise had been of some value for it had established the idea that real awareness of a person means knowing both what they like, how they move, how they behave, what they do and what they say as well as how they speak.

The children should also be encouraged to observe their pets and wild life that live within their local environment, so that they really do perceive and know how a cat washes behind its ears and laps up milk, or how a dog begs, or how a worm writhes and wriggles and disappears into the ground, or how a bird preens its feathers or balances on a fence, or how the class hamster rotates his wheels, jumps onto his cage roof and hangs upside down and swings himself during exercise. So that they are able to recall past observations when they are miming a pet during mime drama or verbal improvisations, they should also begin to note how a branch is weighed down by ripe pears, how some trees have stiff branches which stand out firmly, whilst others sweep down to the ground, perhaps even touching the water in the stream, and how grasses bend and sway as they are wafted by the wind.

The children's attention should also be drawn to the amount of movement which can be observed in a given area. A group might explore the different types of movements which can be seen to be taking place during ten minute eg in the classroom, the school hall, the library or the secretary's office. They may be able to go on a movement discovery walk and collect a list of all the movements they have seen take place during the time that passed from leaving school to returning. A group of seven year olds who went on a movement discovery walk returned with a list including:

Insects crawling in grass and up along flower stems.
Leaves rustled by wind.
Grasses waving and bending.
Smoke curling from factory chimney.
Wheels of traffic turning and traffic travelling.
Traffic signals and belisha light going on and off.
Fish swimming in river.
Movement of water, smooth and slow swirling over weir.
Pedestrians walking and getting onto bus.
Swinging gates.
Child somersaulting on bar.
Child licking ice-cream.

These walks can also serve to help the children realise the number of different incidents which occur in a limited area and which they can utilise during a work out of either verbal or mime drama.

Through sound

The aim of sound awareness is three fold.

1 To draw and focus the children's conscious attention on the different types of sound which can be heard in daily life.
2 To help the children to widen their understanding of sound in relation to music and language.
3 To help the children to realise how sound can be used to provide sound effects in drama or be the basis of a theme for investigations.

The children can begin by simply listening to sounds which can be heard in the classroom.

(a) These are sounds which are actually being made in the room where they are working.
The sound of . . . pencils scratching on paper; a book closed suddenly, sharply, noisily; a clock ticking; the ventilator fan whirling; water running into the sink, or dripping onto a tin lid, or gurgling as it runs down the waste pipe; mice or hamster turning wheel in cage.

(*b*) External sounds which filter into the classroom . . . feet shuffling up and down the corridor; rain on the window pane; tree branch scratching against window pane; typewriter in school office; hooter at nearby factory.

(*c*) External sounds heard during playtime or games lessons . . . ball thudding on bat; footsteps on different surfaces; laughter, crying or yelling; mechanical sounds of nearby pneumatic drill; traffic; dogs barking; chimes of ice cream van.

14 Sensory awareness: sound. Peter listens to the sound of a sea shell

At first the children may simply try to invent mouthed sounds to simulate the noises they have just heard. Then they may make a simple mime exploration of the actions concerned with specific sounds heard in the classroom, ie the actions of writing on paper (using mouthed sounds to simulate pencil scratching). Some children may be able to work out an idea concerned with the use of two or three connected sounds. Thus a child might mime reading a book, close it as he loses interest or is distracted by a fly buzzing overhead, he may try to swot the fly or go to the window and open it and try to drive the fly out.

Next the teacher may be able to draw the children's attantion to the difference in quality of sound; the wail of the siren, the rasp of the hooter, the gentle melodic sweetness of musical chimes, the sharpness of the school bell. She might be able to further their awareness of the length of a note through the comparison of the enduring sustained note of the gong compared with the staccato note of the quickly rung school bell.

Young children might be encouraged to explore their reactions to the sound through making immediate responses to the noises, then they might develop this in movement with a response to sound signals. Older and experienced children might make a simple exploration dance based on an idea which develops out of these specific sound investigations. Others might be encouraged to explore themes based on *Signals* . . . bells heralding school or church time, factory hooters signalling lunch, sirens acting as warning, drums and bugles used as military signals or as scout camp signal. Thus experienced children might explore the theme *Camp* either as a mime or as a verbal drama exploration.

Occasionally the teacher may select one of these specific sounds and use it to introduce the children to an awareness and understanding of 'pitch'. She might recall the ice cream van chime then arrange for the children to listen to, and compare, a variety of chimes, bells and gongs. The children should be encouraged to listen to the variety of sounds made by similar instruments, and their attention should be drawn to the fact that some make high notes and some make low notes, and so develop a feeling for colour, ie tone of sounds. Then the children might be allowed to explore 'pitch' in movement, through free response action or simple mime movement in which they react more gently and quietly and perhaps quickly to the high notes, and slowly and heavily to the low notes.

(d) Body sounds . . . tongue clicking; whistling; smacking lips together; popping side of mouth with finger; singing; finger tapping; foot tapping or stamping; chest thumping or slapping; knee and thigh slapping; hand clapping.

These activities introduce the children to an awareness of sounds which they can make without the use of external implements or instruments and which could be useful for making sound effects for stories, mimes and verbal drama, or could be used as sound stimuli for movement explorations.

The teacher might make up a story that requires sound effects as an integral part of its unfolding and the children themselves may supply the sound effects (using body or mouthed sounds) in the appropriate places. Or the children might supply both the story and the sound effects; either through a straightforward add-on round-robin invention made up by the whole class, with sound effects supplied either by a group of volunteers or the next child in the ring. Or the class can be divided into two groups, one to invent the story and the other group to supply the sound effects. For example, a story invented by a seven-year-old boy provided reasonable scope for the use of body sounds . . . thigh slapping to simulate walking, knee thumping – running, chest slapping – climbing stile, whistling, neighing, lip smacking – nibbling, teeth clicking – galloping, oral ding dongs – bells, wowing noises – dustbin lid rolling, oral blowing – wind, which the children used in the exploration of his story quoted below:

Once upon a time there was a boy. He went for a walk in the country. It was a nice windy day so he walked along slowly until he came to a brook. It was not very wide so he jumped over it. When he got to the other side he found he was in a field so he hurried up to see if he could get out of it. He came to a stile, so he climbed over it onto a road. As he was walking along he saw another field. He stopped to look over the hedge and he saw a horse. He whistled to it and the horse neighed and tossed its head. Then it ran over to the hedge. It nibbled at the hedge, and while it was doing this, the boy climbed onto its back. The horse galloped away. It went up the road and passed a church. The bells were ringing because there was a funeral. All the people were crying because they liked the dead man and they did not want him to be dead. The horse stopped and the boy climbed down and went into the church with the people. So the horse galloped away but it went the wrong way and got into the middle of the town. It was frightened by the traffic. It kicked a dustbin over and the lid fell off and the horse turned round and galloped away and was never seen again.

At the same time the body sounds can be used to introduce the children to the beginning of an understanding of pulse and rhythm through teacher-directed hand clapping and foot stamping activities. For example,

1 The teacher claps a pattern of regular beat, the children listen and try to repeat the exact pattern which the teacher has clapped. (This can be simply three regular claps, at first.) The number of beats can be increased and decreased, until there is a challenge presented – the teacher may clap a five beat pattern, then a six beat pattern and return to a five beat one. The children must listen intently in order to know how many beats are required.

2 The teacher may introduce irregular patterns. This calls for greater concentration when listening and also more skill in memorising and repeating the exact pattern. Simultaneously the children will begin to understand something about phrasing, for an understanding of rhythmic phrasing develops through imitation of good patterns set by the teacher.

3 The teacher introduces a game of question and answer, wherein she claps out a pattern of either regular or irregular beat and the children respond with their own individual response and not a direct imitation of the teacher's exact pattern. Thus the teacher may use an irregular pattern and the children may respond and answer with a pattern of regular beat. An understanding of phrasing or question and answer response can also be developed in movement lessons when the children begin to respond to rhythmic stimuli.

At the same time an awareness for quality of touch might be developed. Gentle taps can be made by bringing the hands together carefully and gently, and loud claps can be made with firm, abrupt hand and arm movements. An understanding of the volume of sound (*crescendo* and *diminuendo*) can also grow out of these activities as the children vary the quality of sound according to their answers. The teacher could continue these investigations in the music lesson using different instruments to emphasise the question and answer. The child might use a castanet to answer a question asked by the teacher's triangle.

INVESTIGATIONS OF ABSTRACT SOUND MADE BY JUNK INSTRUMENTS

These types of sounds are manufactured and made by the children during organised class lessons or during free activity investigations in the music corner, or at the discovery table. The teacher must therefore provide a wide variety of junk materials and encourage the children to use them freely, and also encourage them to bring other materials from home which they can use during their sound experiments.

The materials should include . . . empty tins, cartons, detergent containers, match boxes of various sizes, cheese boxes, cigarette packets, cigar boxes, rubber bands of various sizes and thickness, thin long string, fat short string, gut, elastic of various kinds, old rubber inner tubes, thin tissue papers, thicker cartridge papers, foils, both metal and plastic, waxed papers, sweetie and chocolate papers of the type which hold individual mints, chocolates, toilet rolls, corrugated

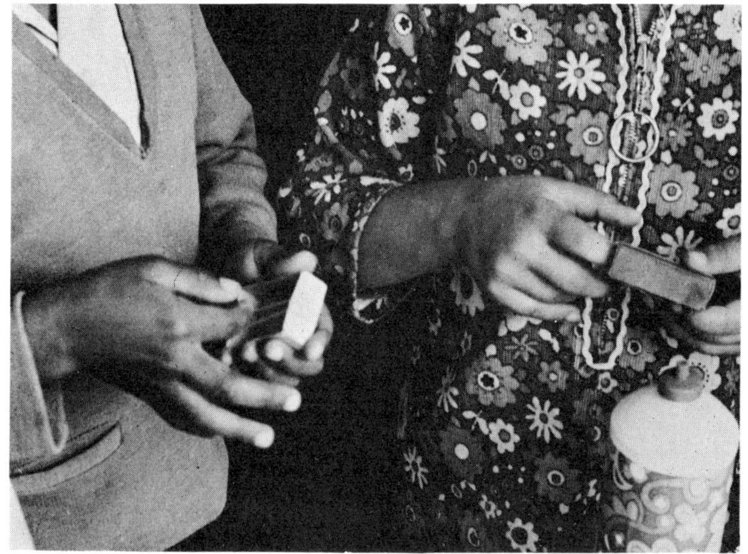

15 *Making junk musical instruments from match boxes*

16 *An assortment of materials for making junk musical instruments*

cardboard, kitchen paper rolls, egg boxes, celluloid, thin plastic sheets, metal strips, cereals and pulses, coffee beans, tea, rice, fir cones, leaves, reeds, grasses, straws, water and assorted bottles, bamboo canes of several thicknesses and sizes, coconut shells, sea shore shells, tooth brushes, combs, discarded broom handles, old pan lids, old pans, plastic and pot basins, wooden spoons, rasps and sandpapers, blocks, bricks, cottonreels, beads, adhesive tape, staples and staplegun.

The children should be encouraged to play and experiment freely in any way they like with the materials, so that they begin to enjoy simply making noises of various kinds and also begin to acquire a discerning awareness of different sounds and know how some of them are made. At the same time, they discover the different quality of sound and volume that results from twanging or banging an instrument or junk instrument; and thus gain an understanding of the different timbres derived from sound producing materials; rubber bands, wood, metals, strings, glass.

Children are often surprised to discover that a discarded detergent container partly filled with coffee beans produces a different kind of sound to that when it is filled with tea. They are intrigued to discover that pitch may vary considerably when they use almost identical materials, that one kind of note can be made with a match box and a thin elastic band, yet, the same match box and a thicker rubber band produces an entirely different note; and that they can actually make two or three notes, if they use the same match box and several different size rubber bands, which will allow them to play a simple tune. They are delighted to find that a ruler, round cheese box and various rubber bands will enable them to make a simple type guitar which will give endless pleasure if they can both play it in school and take it home afterwards.

The children should also be encouraged to discover pitch through blowing through straws of varying lengths so that they may find out for themselves that the longer the straw the higher the note, the shorter the straw, the lower the note. Similarly they might enjoy learning to tune a set of bottles filled with water so that they can play a simple tune.

Older children might be interested in discovering more about the nature of pitch and some of the factors which condition the behaviour of sound. They might be encouraged to stretch a single string between two points over a sounding board, then to pluck it quickly, and listen while the string is allowed to vibrate freely. They might then be allowed to bow it and to listen to the more restricted vibrations as the bow vibrates the string, producing overtones. They can discover that the pitch of the note depends on the thickness of the string, as well as its length, and that the final influence depends on the tightness of the string, also that they can make a similar note with a long piece of thin string as with a short thick piece, although the quality of the short thick string will sound richer than the long thin string.

If they have become interested in discovering vibrations they can listen to those made by a tuning fork when struck and held close to the ear. This can be further extended into an awareness of resonators by filling a jug with water to a certain height, then striking the tuning fork and holding it over the water so that the sound is considerably enriched. If some of the water is poured away or more is added the children can discover that it makes no difference to the original sound.

Some children may be interested to feel vibrations in themselves and should be encouraged to place their fingers lightly on their own throats while they sing a simple tune. Others may listen to the vibrations in a friend's chest while he speaks or sings. And they can discover the vibration of the lip as they play on a simple comb and tissue instrument.

Some children may be surprised to learn that it is possible to see vibrations and may enjoy seeing their voice dance on an oscilloscope, if one can be made available. Others may try to make a simple voice print by making a home-made apparatus, which may form a stimulus for a movement exploration. Other children might try to make a simple phonograph with a paper cone, pin and old record turntable. And all the children should be allowed to make simple wind sound-sculptures for themselves using metals, glass, wood and strings. These could be linked with art mobiles as an extension of visual awareness activities and also in turn might provide a basis for a creative dance theme.

Thus it becomes obvious that although the provision of ample materials are necessary and that plenty of free play discovery should be allowed, it is most important that the teacher should be careful to see that the investigations are deepened enough through arranging situations wherein the children can discover information for themselves. It is also essential that she makes sure that very young children do not only become so fascinated with the simpler task of putting things into containers and taking them out again that they do not bother to listen to the kind of sound which the container and its contents might have produced. It is useful therefore if the teacher prepares several junk instruments and sound containers which she can allow the children to use during story time as sound effects, or simply use to discover what kind of noise they make, so that they actually do hear a variety of different sounds and noises and may thus be stimulated to want to make their own sound instrument. It must be emphasised, however, that the teacher-prepared containers need to be adequately fastened with glue, tape and screwtops, so that the more curious children will have difficulty in opening them and thus be deterred from trying to empty out what is inside, to see what really makes the noise. Otherwise the containers would become empty and soon become useless, as one distressed student discovered on teaching practice. It can be helpful if the teacher actually makes up some sound containers in front of the children, so that they can see, step by step, what is inside each one, and cease to be curious about what is making the noise. They will prove to be a useful addition to classroom apparatus, for they have endless possibilities either as junk instruments (which can be used as an adequate introduction to percussion band work), or as additional instruments, or as sound containers (useful for sound effects for stories, poems, mimes and verbal drama improvisations), or as sound signals for simple movement response exploration or as instruments which the children can use to accompany themselves during creative dance or a sensation response stimulus for art work.

MUSIC CORNER

While the children are experimenting with making simple junk instruments and becoming aware of the sounds which these instruments make, they should be allowed to experiment freely with percussion instruments. This should take place during teacher controlled work with small groups, for instruments are expensive and the idea must be inculcated that they are musical instruments and not toys. The music corner should contain tambourines, castanets, triangles, cymbals, sleigh bells, drums, claves, tubular bells, glockenspiel chime bars and a xylophone.

The children should be shown the correct way to hold the instruments and also how to play them. They should be allowed to discover the exact sound which each instrument makes, and should be encouraged to discover the limitations and possibilities of each instrument.

They should use them to discover volume and strength and to study pulse, pattern, and rhythmic phrasing. It is essential that they really begin to understand and develop an awareness of pulse. Pulse is a universal in life. They can experience it in the body during awareness discovery activities, through feeling their own heart beating and should realise that it is a steady, regular beat fundamental to life. Equally they should realise that pulse is fundamental and essential both in music and movement. It is the basic unit of rhythm and can be varied, being regular and irregular. At first they should explore regular pulse (one group might play a steady regular beat while the others can move to it in a movement locomotion exercise). Next they should explore irregular pulse, strong accented pulses, played at irregular intervals. The group of children who are exploring free movement should be allowed to respond freely. Next the children should be led to realise that pulses are put together in groups of 2, 3, 4 units. These units are called bars. They should explore moving to a 4 bar unit and should be led to understand that the first unit is the leader. This is emphasised by accenting the first unit in each bar when playing. Thus in movement the response to the first unit will be firmer and with more weight. *Jump,* run, run, run, *Jump,* run, run, run. Next they should realise that several bars are put together to form a phrase. They should explore a simple phrase in movement. Similarly, they should understand that several phrases are put together to form a whole sentence and children experienced in movement should explore putting several phrases together to form a movement sentence, eg, the children can fit together uncurling, growing and locomotion or elevation phrases.

They should discover pitch through experiments with tuned instruments because these instruments produce sounds of definite graded pitch which can easily be differentiated and heard. They should explore pitch in movement. An octave should be played and the children should curl up in a ball and grow slowly upright as the music travels up the octave, they should sink downwards as the music returns to base. Older children might be led to realise that variations in pitch allow melody to be formed.

They should be encouraged to explore the dynamic quality of music, linking the exploration with movement. Next they should explore tone in music and should be led to realise that tonality is the relationship of one note to another. At the same time their investigation of tone might be linked with their art work. They might be encouraged to make a tone painting or pattern. Later they might try to express in sound, something of the nature of their picture. Very young reception children might simply try to paint their immediate reaction to the sound, it will be neither a painting nor a pattern but simply an emotion doodle, perhaps made with a paint stick, so that the child is able to have the means to express his reaction immediately to hand. Sometimes, older children might make a doodle with a paint stick then try to explore his visual doodle in the music corner, trying out various junk instruments to find one which might best fit the shape, tone and mood of his visual symbol. Some children might try to invent a doodle symbol and explore it in dance, and invent a junk instrument which can make the right kind of sound to accompany their dance.

ORAL AWARENESS: SINGING

Singing plays a valuable part in developing children's awareness of sounds, words and music. Young children respond quickly to nursery rhymes, counting songs, simple folk songs and singing games. They are happy to listen to the teacher singing and love to join in as they learn the words. Older children enjoy songs which permit antiphonal singing. Songs therefore provide ample opportunity for the exploration of pitch, phrasing, speed, volume and tone. The activity is enjoyable and most children join in joyfully when asked to do so. This is useful, for young children can be encouraged to sing a song in an appropriate place during the unfolding of a tale, eg a lullaby as mother is rocking baby to sleep, which heightens the dramatic effect of the story.

Older children who already possess a wide repertoire of songs should be encouraged to break into song during a verbal drama exploration. Often in fact, well known playground jingles or singing games can be the starting point for a verbal drama theme. Equally, they are useful in movement. Even shy children join in singing games willingly. The simple set patterns are easy to remember and they learn them quickly. The activity is pleasurable because they are not required to use their imagination to invent a creative response. Though resourceful children who are imaginative, often try to improve on the singing game or invent a slightly different kind of dance. The children enjoy the activity and at the same time are being helped to learn to work with a group or partner, and often this enables them to move more easily into group or partner work in creative movement.

ORAL AWARENESS: SPOKEN

These activities are concerned with making the children aware of spoken sound. If the children are to benefit from the activity they need to be relaxed. Therefore it is useful to commence the involvement with simple breathing exercises which aid relaxation and reduce tension. At the same time, learning to breathe slowly helps to foster the idea of slowness and some children are encouraged to speak more slowly. Gradually, it helps the children to acquire the ability to take in an adequate supply of breath and thus be able to sing and speak without gasping. The children should be asked to lie down or stand up and place hands, palm down, with thumbs and fingers resting on base of ribs. They should breathe in through *nose* with mouth closed, then expell the breath slowly through the mouth, or sometimes breathe out quickly and forcibly through mouth making *ahhh* sound.

This exercise should be followed by relaxation exercises.

1 The children should stand or sit. Drop head slightly forward on to chest. They should murmur *mmmm*. Repeating *mmmm* as they travel up and down an octave. They should beat the chest gently in rhythm with sound, and vary the exercise by murmuring *nnnn*. They should be encouraged to feel the vibration of the lips.
They should sit, drop head forward and roll it around. Drop head backwards and roll to starting position. Raise head. Repeat opposite way.

Next they should explore exercises leading towards clearer speech. They should be seated around teacher in a group. The teacher should say the exercises first so that the children can see the correct mouth positions.

Exercises for tongue to promote clearer articulation.

1 Rest tip of tongue on lower lip. Stretch upwards and outwards so that it becomes pointed and the very tip of tongue makes a neat point.
2 Raise tongue to centre of upper lip, move downwards with slow deliberate action until tongue touches centre lower lip. Repeat several times.
3 Move tongue from side to side slowly and deliberately touching corners of mouth.
4 Move tongue in a completely circular movement.
5 Protrude tongue out of mouth, pushing it slowly until fully stretched, withdraw it quickly and roll up to touch roof of mouth. Repeat several times.

EXERCISES FOR THE LIPS

Good voice production occurs when the lips alternate flexibly between two main positions, relaxed and closed with no backward stretching of corners, and fully rounded, pouting forwards. It is essential that the exercises be performed so that all the surface cheek muscles which actually control lip movement are fully stretched and exercised.

1 Close mouth with lower lip slightly behind upper lip. Press lips firmly together. Release, without separating lips.
2 Press lips together firmly, smile broadly, purse lips into prominent pout, smile, release and relax lips.
3 Blow lips forward so they bounce making raspberry sound.

EXERCISES FOR JAW

There are two main positions for exercising the lower jaw. Neutral, relaxed position suitable for saying *eee,* and dropped position suitable for saying *ahhh.* The exercise is based on alternate repetition of *oo – ay – eee – ah – aw – oo – ay – ee – ah – aw.*

The elements of pitch, stress and speed are just as important in speech as they are in song, and the children should explore them through repetitive chanting. As the children have just explored the sound *oo – ay – ee – ah – aw,* they can develop this kind of chanting into an exploration of all the phonetic sounds of the alphabet, *aaa, bbb, ccc,* etc. They can link two sounds together *aa – bb – aa – bb* speeding up delivery to form *aabbaabbaabbaabb.* Invariably this leads some children to notice that the sound is somewhat similar to alibaba. This can be chanted and the children can hear that they have moved from an abstract sound to an actual word. One child was so intrigued by this discovery that she drew a picture of herself chanting her name and Alibaba chanting his! The exercise had provided the child with an unusual form of stimulation which found its end product in art. As Alibaba is a name, it is a natural progression from this if the children begin to explore the sound of their own names.

1 The children should be encouraged to call out their names and the children repeat the sound and name until everybody's first name has been sounded. Attention should be drawn to the syllabic stress – Ann, one stress; Peter, two stresses; Amanda, three stresses; Sebastian, four stresses. Then the children can repeat their names again exploring the dynamic quality of sound, beginning quietly and reaching crescendo then gradually sinking down to diminuendo.
2 They should make up chanting jingles based on names – Ann, Peter, Dominic, Paul, Ann, Peter, Dominic, Paul.
3 Next they should explore the individual sound arrangement pattern of their full names, i.e. forename against surname – Kathryn Goldie, Christopher Clapperton, Billy Brown, Paul Lowndes – chanting and clapping to emphasise the stresses. This can be linked with pulse and pattern awareness in music, using junk or percussion instruments or, if chime bars are used, two distinct notes should be played so that children can hear their names through pitch.
4 They can explore any amount of subject themes through chanting names of flowers, towns, streets, birds, instruments.
5 Similarly, they should be encouraged to find out local street cries, 'coal', 'rags and bones', 'papers', 'milk', etc. Playground jingles too

should be explored as these make the exercise enjoyable and give extended awareness of pace, emphasise rhythm, stress pattern and vocabulary. No attempt should be made to try to alter the children's natural pronunciation through the mistaken belief that they are not speaking BBC English. Local dialects are part of our heritage and often add pleasing individuality to personality. This does not mean that attention cannot be drawn in passing to slovenly speech, bad articulation, over mouthing, or what is or is not grammatically correct.

6 They should explore tongue twisters, eg One old Oxford ox – (Puffin book of nursery rhymes) (Opie).

7 The children should now progress to free choice of words. They should choose a word that appeals to them and chant it, eg 'tomato'. They should repeat it varying the speed of delivery in varying degrees of melodic phrasing, speaking normally, whispering softly, shouting. Often, this is the time to explain that it is just as important to be able to speak really quietly as well as loudly. Some children become discouraged because they cannot speak loudly and project their voice across a room. They need to be praised that they do well in whispering exercises so that their confidence is restored.

8 The children should be encouraged to make up a simple phrase that has a particular emotive appeal for them. No comment should be made about the originality of the suggestion (though rude words should be discouraged of course!). One six year old immigrant child was enamoured with the thoughts and words of purple pancakes. The idea was taken up enthusiastically by the class and when the chanting/clapping exercise was over, a discussion arose around the topic, which led one child to invent a story about a pancake . . .

> 'There was once a captain who loved pancakes so he called up the ship's cook and told him to make him one. So the cook got some eggs and some milk and some flour and mixed them all together and made it, and when it was ready he panked it up and down but it missed the pan and fell onto the floor and got dirty, and covered in hairs, so the captain threw it overboard. It started to sink but a little fish saw it and caught hold of it and towed it to the bottom of the sea. He rested the pancake on two stones so that it could be the roof of his little house and keep the rain out. He swam underneath it and he was very happy. But one day another fish came and bit a hole in one end of the pancake and it floated away to the top of the sea. Then as it was

> going along a frog saw it so he jumped on board and sailed it far far away (for ever).'

In this case the exercise had ended finally with the stimulation of several children's imagination and culminated in this rather imaginative verbal end product. Indeed, the discussions and comments that follow up a particular exercise often prove to be of equal value, for they help the children to think and to re-organise their reactions and ideas quickly and to communicate these spontaneously. This is very valuable training that proves its usefulness in later verbal improvisation workouts, for often these discussions release the children's inhibitions about confiding ideas, beliefs, or thoughts which interest them. Indeed one child who had never spoken out for a whole term suddenly, after involvement in exercises that consisted of explorative chanting of animals, names, etc, confided that she had previously lived in Aden. Lizards had often crept into their house and they had found them everywhere in the kitchen, bedroom and living room and one had crawled underneath the carpet and her father, not knowing it was there, had trodden on it and squashed it into a slimy wet mess. She had felt free to suddenly communicate this information which immediately interested the others and led to unexpected responses as two boys began to writhe and thrash about on the floor (simulating, as they said, 'being squashed crocodiles' squirming before they were dead). And this in turn provoked interest in a nature lesson about lizards and newts and led to the making of several junk experiments concerned with animal representations.

This sudden awareness that they are free to communicate and speak out is the first important discovery in drama work. It is the establishment of this feeling of freedom to project their ideas and themselves that is necessary for later successful participation in worthwhile drama explorations. Once this feeling of security is established (that what they say will not be considered worthless or provoke ridicule and laughter), the children become more confident and are able and willing to talk and discuss and perhaps pass judgements.

A six year old girl told how she had witnessed a fight in a furniture store:

> I was in Wood Green with my mummy and aunty. We went in the shop to buy a wardrobe and when we were coming out we heard a noise so we turned round and we saw two ladies fighting. Handbags were flying and hats were flying and money was flying about all over the place. And they were screaming and screaming. And a black man was looking on and his mouth was wide open. He must have been thinking 'They may be fighting in my country, but they are fighting in this one too'.

A comment about social behaviour . . . and one which the children followed up with the comment that people always seem to be fighting and that Dr Martin Luther King had been killed by similar impetuous people. (It was just after his assassination.) So an exercise that was meant to facilitate sound and word awareness ended with a much deeper moral context.

The children should be encouraged to remember such incidents and to mention them in class, so that they can be compiled into the classroom book of 'Recorded Incidents'. The records can either be copied or written into the collection by the children who are able to write or they can be copied in by the teacher. The children can make drawings or paintings and so further explore their descriptions of the incidents which they have witnessed, eg try to recall their impressions or to express their comments about the incident. The children who are art-shy can collect images cut from magazines and use these to make a collage comment or description of an incident. The book can later serve as a basis for themes which can be explored either in mime or verbal improvisations. Often when nursery and reception age children 'think aloud' their comments are revealing and pertinent. During a journey in the Lake District a young child stared hard first through a side window and then through the back window of the car. Suddenly she remarked to herself . . . 'That mountain is peeping through the trees at me, it will kill me if we stop and sit down'. This sense of foreboding had been conditioned by a cloud which suddenly passed in front of the sun which dramatically highlighted one side of the mountain so that it appeared large, dark and craggy, yet this was unnoticed by her twin sister. Later on the return journey her twin sister was overheard talking and happily chanting to herself about the procession of oncoming traffic. Quite unconsciously she fitted her words to the speed of the cars whizzing past, so her child chatter developed a strong rhythmic speed which echoed exactly the flow of the traffic. Her chatter was noted down and is reproduced below, exactly as she said it . . .

> One, one, one two, one two three, four, red, blue car blue car, blue black black green, yellow lorry, yellow lorry yellow lorry, yellow lorry yellow lolly, yellow lolly yellow lolly, yellow lollipop, want a lolly, want a lolly, want a yellow lollipop, want a –, Is that cow dead down there?

Children often make up similar jingles which they happily chant for hours on end. Often they can be encouraged to include the jingles in verbal improvisations.

Playground jingles, nursery rhymes and traditional poems can often provide an adequate introduction to poetry.

Children need to hear poetry as often as possible. At the same time they need to hear it in a situation which will allow them to be receptive to the poems. For this reason, time set apart for class poetry lessons, when the children hear five or six poems read by the teacher is often less useful than a method which allows the children to hear only one or two poems during the total context of the day's work. For instance, they will better appreciate two poems about nature if they are read to them at the end of a nature lesson. They will really 'hear' the poems and respond to them far more at this time. The poems will also be more meaningful, and their response will be deepened if the poems are subsequently explored in the movement or art lessons, eg if the nature lesson is about caterpillars and butterflies, the movement poem 'Caterpillars' from *Poems for Movement,* would provide an interesting stimulus, and later in art lesson, mobiles, murals and paintings and prints could be explored based on caterpillars or on butterfly wings.

At the same time, they might be encouraged to invent a simple movement poem for themselves, eg a seven year old wrote . . .

I saw a little worm
Wriggling on the ground
It wriggled and wriggled
And wriggled and wriggled
Then it curled itself around.

Similarly, poems based on the theme *colour,* should be heard when the children have just been involved in colour discovery explorations. During a discussion which followed on free activity choice work, when the children had been concerned with finding out basic facts about colour, tone, the dominant and recessive colour behaviour, a group of seven year olds were asked what the colours 'meant' to them Which colours they liked best and why. Then they were asked to say what they immediately thought of when a particular colour was mentioned. It was suggested that their answers should be collated into a 'poem' called 'Colour', which would be written down and put up on the wall in the book corner. The children were interested. Each child chose a different colour. They were asked to think about it, then their replies were noted down.

Yellow is a newly painted door.
Green is my aunty's teeth.
Blue is Easter.
Black is shadows dancing on the wall.
White is clean shirts waving on the washing line.
Orange is tall chimney pots.
Red is creative writing.

The last response surprised the teacher. She asked the child what had led her to make this statement. The child replied 'Well my creative writing book has a red cover, and you let me use my red biro to write in it, and I don't use my red biro for other work, so I thought red is creative writing'.

As the children were keen to have their work read to the class and it was convenient, the teacher called the class together. The children showed their art work to the rest of the class, then they stood in a line and each child said his particular statement about colour. Often this kind of free verbal communication work helps shy children to get used to speaking in front of others, pride in their immediate success in other work helps them to overcome self-consciousness. Then the teacher read two poems from the book *Adventure in Colour* by Mary O'Neill 'World Work Series' and also Kandinsky poem 'Bassoon'.

Often poems which are meant for adults or older children contain a narrative verse which younger children can understand. It can be useful to read this verse to them, to extend their imagination, feeling for words and vocabulary. Poetry has a unique appeal for most children, they respond to the hilarious humour of nonsense poems, to the beauty of clear cut and expressive sentences and phrases, to the vivid images and to beauty of sound and rhythm. They can enjoy hearing, learning, reciting and chanting the poems and jingles. Many children never hear poetry outside school, except nursery rhymes or playground jingles. It is essential therefore to allow them to enjoy all kinds of poetry.

Some older children are afraid of poetry. Often they have been led to believe it is a special kind of language. They often think that it must rhyme and have a regular metre so they are afraid to try to write or make up poems for themselves. Often it is a revelation to learn that Hughes Mearns said 'poetry is when you talk to yourself'. Many children do just that and they can be heard many times a day talking and chanting to themselves, they make up little jingles about something which interests them or which can accompany some action they are performing, and are quite unaware that they are unconsciously inventing a very simple poem. This should be brought to their attention. Often it can be noted down and can be copied out by the child so that he can feel he is successful in handling words. The word 'poem' may be a grand word but he has taken another step towards creative verbal work.

Poetry and movement poems provide a different form of involvement with poetry. The work links up verbal awareness with creative movement activities. Simultaneously, the children can further extend and widen their vocabulary and increase their awareness of expressive phrases and feeling for words. They can enjoy responding mentally and physically to the sound of the language, to the vivid images and to the various rhythms of the poem. As their experience in this kind of involvement grows, their response will become more varied and increasingly sensitive and more imaginative as they learn to control and manipulate their limbs and whole body. Their interest in the work will deepen gradually, for the poems generally allow the children to find their own means of creative expression and at the same time develop their powers of perception. Some poems allow for contrasts between high and low movements, others encourage the children to move about and utilise all the available open space. Some introduce the children to variations of pace and speed, others concentrate on simple repetitive actions. Some encourage the children to use the whole body fully in broad expansive movements perhaps after slowly unfolding the body or before curling up into a tightly rolled ball shape, others encourage them to move with small refined movements, or with particular parts of the body only. Some poems allow for simple characterisation. Two books which are extremely useful for this kind of work are *Skipping Susan* and *Poems for movement* by E. J. M. Woodland, published by Evans Brothers.

The traditional poem, '*What's your name*', provides straightforward question and answer conversation. '*Gossip*' helps them to see how to form a conversation which gives direct information about self and which also seems to invoke a life continued elsewhere, which they have just left and to which they will return. A wide repertoire of poetry can therefore be of enormous value to children. They can enjoy the poems simply for themselves. They hear and come across new words in a natural way and they can gather the meaning of unusual new words through the way the poet has used them in the text, so their vocabulary is gradually widened. At the same time they can hear how words fit together to form precise and expressive phrases or sentences and thus they can lean to fit words together to make express phrases of their own invention which they can use in creative writing, normal conversation and improvised drama.

4 Body awareness

Awareness of the body can be best experienced first through touch, when one part of the body is pressed against another part, or when the body is pressed against an unyielding surface. The pressure exerted by the surface focuses attention on part of the body area and awareness of the particular part of the body is emphasised. At the same time the children can learn the name of the particular body part.

They can also become aware of their size and shape if they are encouraged to make life size two dimensional paper sculptures of themselves during art lessons, which they can utilise in murals.

Body awareness can be further experienced through activity, during expressive movement when the children explore using their bodies as a creative vehicle, or during the exploration of teacher directed exercises. They hear, notice and learn the words as the teacher draws attention to the parts and to the activities. If the teacher writes the words on cards which she holds up as she says the words, the children may learn to read the words at the same time. At first these words may simply be the body parts, *leg, arm*. Later she may use two cards, one showing the locomotion command and the other the body part, *jump, toes*. Cards emphasising the space aspect could also be shown, *jump, high; run, far-away*.

The exercises which are included in this section help the children to become more consciously aware of their own body. They also help to introduce the children to some of the fundamental elements of creative movement, body shape, relationships, space aspect and the aspect of effort. At the same time the concept of balance can be brought to their attention, for some of the exercises require the children to explore balancing the weight of the body on various parts of the body when standing, sitting, lying, kneeling. This is important for an understanding of balance and weight transference is fundamental to movement activities.

Because young children quickly become bored with formal exercises, the teacher should select one or two which focus attention on a particular aspect of body awareness which she intends to explore during the lesson. Then perhaps five minutes of the lesson should be spent in consciously exploring the exercises formally, and the remainder of the lesson should be concerned with using the information gathered during a more creative sequence.

BREATHING EXERCISES

Young reception children are too young to be introduced to consciously controlled breathing exercises but they can benefit from the state of calmness induced by the process of lying down and simply breathing in a normal manner. At the same time, they can discover something about the body through feeling the active movement of the breathing process and the heart beat.

They should lie down on their backs on the floor, eyes closed, and breathe in and out normally, and try to relax. They should place their hands on their chests, fingers just touching and feel the chest rise and fall as breath is drawn in and expelled.

Older children can explore the exercises more consciously.

1 Lie down with back on floor. Place hands palm downwards on chest, fingers just touching. Breathe in slowly. Feel body swell. Hold breath, then either breathe out quickly through mouth or sometimes slowly through nose.

17 *Relaxation*

2 Lie down. Place hands on lower ribcage, palms downwards. Breathe in deeply, feel fingers move apart as body swells. Hold breath. Breathe out quickly through mouth.

3 Lie down. Move hands to side of body, breathe in slowly, feel sideways extension of body. Hold breath, breathe out slowly through nose.
4 Lie down, place hands cup tummy, thumbs touching over navel, feel rise and fall of body as breath is drawn in and expelled.
5 Purse lips, blow up cheeks, exhale air slowly, feel cheeks fall.

SELF AWARENESS EXERCISES

Lying on floor

1 Lie down, body fully extended, sometimes face downwards, sometimes on back, head resting on folded hands. Relax as much as possible, letting limbs and muscles sag. Note relationship of body to floor, feeling hardness of floor against specific parts as directed by teacher, tummy, knees etc. Experience relationship of head on arms, noting softness of arms compared with hard floor under body.
2 Tauten entire body, move arms to lie on floor above head. Keep legs straight, point toes so that body is lying in long horizontal thin straight line, stretch body so that the muscles are pulling as they stretch. Relax gradually, until body is saggy. Relax completely. Try to wriggle relaxed body about on floor. Then spread arms and legs out wide and feel 'openness' of body shape.
3 Curl up into tight ball shape, feel nearness of limb to limb. (Closing aspect of movement). Relax, uncurl slowly, move body into totally different shape, angular or twisted to begin to re-explore new body shape and its relationship to floor. Sit up slowly.

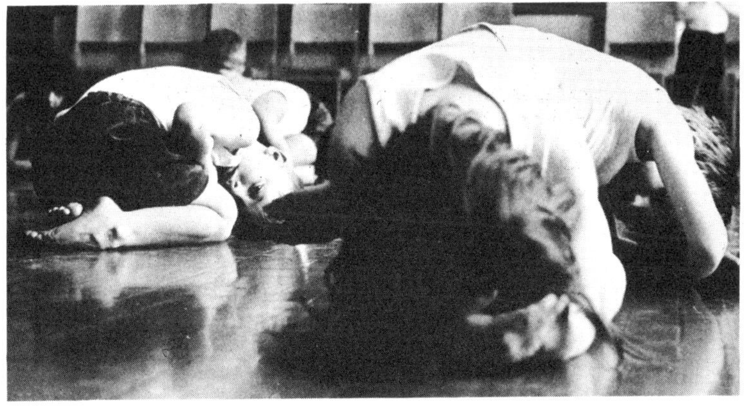

18 Curling up into balls

4 Lie down, with back of head resting on floor. Relax, close eyes, focus attention on sounds that can be heard in room, or in corridor outside. Focus attention on self. Rock head slightly from side to side. Experience hardness of floor through pressing body parts consciously against it. Bend legs onto tummy, so that head and trunk are taking weight of body. Lower legs slowly. Stretch out into thin shape, stretch fingers and toes to enhance stretching process. Feel pull of muscles and experience lessening of contact with floor. Relax.

5 Lie down normally, experience length of body by flexing muscles slowly beginning with wriggling toes and work towards head. Relax, and wriggle head, then flex muscles from shoulders down to toes.

6 Lie down, turn onto side, arm extended on floor above head. Head resting on arm, feet pointed in straight line, make body as thin as possible. Feel hardness of floor under hip and shoulder in particular. Try to compare width of body when lying on side with that when lying on body front. (Draw round it to emphasise width of floor area taken up by body in these two different positions).

Sitting

1 Sit down on floor. Keep legs straight out in front, feel hardness of floor under bottom and backs of legs and heels. Beat floor with heels and calves.

2 Cross legs, feel difference in contact with floor, concentrate on self. Roll and drop head backwards and forwards and sideways. Shake arms and wrists. Flick fingers open and shut. Explore body through tapping. Feel spine. Wriggle and rotate trunk. Place hands on floor, close to hips and try to lever body off floor, feel thrust and tension in arms. Beat floor with hands and clap them above head, vigorously, relax.

3 Change position to sit with knees under chin. Make body shape as enclosed and as small as possible. Try to focus attention on self, then on object across room.

4 Hang-sit on climbing nets, feel weight of body hanging on arms, feel tactile surface of net under curled toes or foot or on thighs if legs are slipped through ropes.

5 Sit on chair in classroom, note where body presses against its hard surfaces.

BODY AWARENESS THROUGH TOUCH

1 Explore fingers, rubbing fingers of one hand against fingers on

same hand. Explore both hands. Let fingers press hard together, move apart slowly, come together slowly with light touch. Explore total hand and move up wrists, along arms to shoulders. Let hands come together quickly, loud clap, firm movement. Grasp hands firmly and feel hardness of bones. Press hands together and feel pressure on palms. Close hands tightly, allow to pop open suddenly, stretch fingers widely then close slowly, open one by one, then close quickly together. Let fingers rotate around each other, then hands.

2 Feel toes with fingers, then explore whole foot and legs.
3 Explore one foot with other foot, travelling up leg.
4 Explore surfaces of body with nose, ear, forehead, chin, cheek.

When the children have become interested in the various parts of the body, it is possible to extend their interest into an awareness of how the various parts of the body can be used to convey and express simple impressions through mime.

Thus children who have been exploring hand, arm and fingers can be encouraged to invent a simple mime conversation for two children, eg the actions might include waving the arms about to catch someone's attention, Stop, come over here, Who me? Yes, you, No! I am going on that way, Please come, Why? Please, (shrug), Please, OK, Come quietly, shhh!

19 Shirley and Fotoula practising hand awareness

Or all the children can explore a sequence based on a movement poem concerned with a flower opening in sunshine and closing at nightfall.

Or they might investigate a theme based on darning a sock, Pick up needle, thread it carefully, pick up sock, wriggle hand into and arrange it. Begin to darn, remembering to extend arm as thread is pulled through. Twist hands about as sock is turned for cross weaving. Cut wool with scissors.

Similarly, those who have just explored foot awareness can explore mimes based on planting a seed, flattening soil with hands and feet, breaking stick with foot and digging actions. Or they can explore a theme allied to locomotion awareness, eg going for a walk in the woods.

1 Sit down, pull imaginary socks on, put on shoes, tie laces.
2 Set off, travelling happily.
3 Stumble, foot is hurt, ankle might be twisted or they might have blister or stone in shoes.
4 Sit down, examine hurt foot, taking shoes and sock off. If blister or twisted foot, hop or hobble home; if stone, remove it, then redress and walk on.

BODY AWARENESS WHEN STANDING

These exercises allow the children to explore body awareness and balance, and help them to become aware of kinesphere and their relationship to space.

1 Stand erect, balanced, arms by side, soles of feet flat on floor. Feel hardness of floor. Shift weight onto one foot, then onto other foot, slowly, so that weight of body is really experienced on one foot. Push feet into floor. Lift one leg, balance, raise heels off ground, lower leg and stand firmly on two feet. Move feet wider apart so that weight transference is more consciously felt as body swings further over from side to side and the children can really experience the rock and tilt.
2 Stand normally, rock backwards and forwards on the feet, slowly, emphasising balancing on heels, then on toes.
3 Stand normally, sink slowly into crouch position. Raise arms slowly above head letting them lead body upwards until it is stretched, pushing upwards into a pin shape. Focus attention on hands. Look at ceiling and focus attention on it. Focus attention on hands again. Lower arms to enfold body making it as narrow as possible. Stretch arms outwards and focus attention on object across room. Raise one arm, focus attention on it and lunge body forward, bending one knee, move into thrusting arrow shape.

Feel energy going into the thrusting action, hold position. Focus attention out of body, then on hand again and return to basic body position. Move feet wide apart, raise arms above head, wide apart and experience broad shape, lower body to crouch position, turn feet outwards.

EXERCISE FOR AWARENESS AND RELAXATION AND FLOW

Stand tall, feet close together, extend arms above head. Let fingers sag into wrists, then let wrists sag into forearms. Let arms droop into shoulders, head sag and drop onto chest. Let head lead dropping process downwards, upper body sagging and dropping forwards, hands dropping, hanging loosely. Wriggle hips, let thighs begin to sag and knees bend. Lower leg, sag until body is completely relaxed and can fall down quite safely onto floor.

EXERCISE TO EXPERIENCE TENSION

Stand up, with arms by side. Without moving foot position, begin to tauten body muscles upwards from toes, through feet to ankles. Lower legs, press knees back firmly, then thighs, straighten hips and spine, press shoulders back, flex and tauten arm muscles. Hold neck firm, raise chin. Then begin to relax and sag.

EXERCISE FOR LIMBERING UP THROUGH SHAKING

Stand normally. Shake left leg, then right leg. Then with both feet on ground, rotate feet, wriggle hips and rotate upper body, shake shoulders, arms and hands and head. Alternately loosen up by keeping legs straight, swing alternate legs from hip like pendulum, backwards, forwards and sideways. When legs feel loosened, stand with feet wide apart, weight on ball of foot. Bend knees slightly, thrust hip out from side to side, let arms flap. Shake whole body.

BODY AWARENES THROUGH LIFTING

1 Stand erect, balanced. Raise arms sideways, allowing arms to glide upwards and outwards until level with shoulders. Lower arms slowly, floating downwards.
2 Stand erect, raise arms sideways, level with shoulders. Bend arms keeping hand level with shoulders. Thrust arms out sideways or forwards. Lower quickly.
3 Stand erect, balanced, raise arms sideways above head, keeping arms in line with ears. Stretch fingers, pointing to ceiling. Hold stretched position, feeling pull from waist. Try to keep the

'stretch' as arms are lowered down sideways. This gives a good posture position.

4 Stand erect. Raise arms forward, slashing upwards quickly. Hold at shoulder level. Push arms into space in front of body, continue slashing upwards overhead. Lower quickly.

5 Stand erect, rotate arms around body with circular motion. Arms travelling forwards, backwards or across body, either with vigorous rhythm or with slow considered motion.

6 Raise shoulders, hunch around neck, drop with sudden strong action, feeling pull downwards.

7 Stand erect, raise arms to shoulder height, bend arms letting forearms dangle downwards. Shake. Reverse position so that arms point upwards to ceiling, elbows still at shoulder level. Lower left arm to point downwards, keeping right arm pointing to ceiling, alternate positions.

8 Raise arms and explore sequences of combined speeds and rhythm shooting upwards, thrusting sideways, slashing downwards, floating upwards, flicking fingers, quivering hands, press arms into space.

Legs

9 Stand with feet close together, lift one leg sideways to hip height, lower slowly, keeping balance.

10 Stand erect, feet slightly apart, lift leg, extending it forward or backwards exploring space, push into space, lower slowly, stopping to explore different height levels.

11 Lie down on side, take weight of body on hip and elbow. Lift one leg, let it glide through air, exploring space, lower slowly.

12 Lie down with back on floor. Raise two legs quickly, bend onto tummy, thrust alternate legs into air, bicycling motion. Stop, with both legs extended in air, lower together, keeping legs straight. Place arms above head. Lower to floor, feel stretch throughout body, move arms to side, relax.

13 Lie down on tummy. Raise body quickly lifting arms and legs off floor. Hold position. Lower limbs quickly and relax.

14 Lie down with back on floor. Raise knees keeping feet flat on floor, lift hips, taking weight of body on shoulders. Hold, then lower body.

15 Lie down on back, place hands above head, raise hips and knee so body assumes crab position, arch back, hold, lower slowly.

16 Crouch down, keep hands on floor and straighten legs, bend quickly into crouch position.

5 Locomotion

Most children enjoy moving about and are adept at finding ways of exploring the possibilities of travelling around a given area, and, given the invitation to explore an open space, will generally do so by a method of locomotion that is fast and energetic, running and skipping, rather than walking, for most children find slow movement activities less exciting. Walking seems to be too ordinary an activity, yet they are quick to develop enjoyment of this kind of exploration once their attention is drawn to the fact that it is possible to vary the quality and actual method of walking through speed, flow, weight and gait. It is therefore essential to help children to build up a wide knowledge of ways in which they can travel and at the same time induce a feeling for quality in movement.

It is desirable that the children should wear only vest and underpants so that they are not hampered by restrictive outer garments. It is also desirable that they work barefooted. They are less likely to slip and fall, and their feet have more flexible mobility and have a more sensitive response to the surface on which they are working.

STAGE ONE

Young reception children should be allowed simply to explore all the methods of locomotion that are possible; walking, running, crawling, skipping, hopping, jumping, leaping, rolling, travelling forwards, backwards, and sideways at various height levels, on their bottoms, tummies, knees, as well as on their feet. They enjoy working to piano accompaniment and if this is possible the work can be linked with music awareness training. They should be encouraged to explore the dynamic quality of music, moving with slow heavy steps in response to low notes, and use flexible quiet steps to the high notes. They should explore a curved pathway either along the ground or in air space, responding to the high and low notes, loud and soft sounds, staccato or sustained notes, varying their speed to the rhythm and the beat. They should be allowed to travel about freely, starting from a position near to the teacher and should be encouraged to return near to her, as this helps to foster the idea of converging and dispersing which is used in later creative dance. They should be encouraged to explore all the space in the room and to spread out and not bunch closely together during the exploration, following their own nose rather than the direction of a friend, so that they become resourceful in their own right and develop a sense of confidence when moving around. If they are encouraged to invent mouthed sound to accompany some of their movements they can extend the exercise into a simple mime investigation. Thus an exploration of travelling backwards and forwards in short spurts accompanied by appropriate sounds can be developed into an investigation of a theme about 'shunting trains'. This is turn could be enlarged into an exploration of the theme 'a journey'. Occasionally they should be allowed to travel across a variety of surfaces during an exploration, and perhaps travel along an uneven surface, with one foot on the floor and the other on a low bench. Sometimes they might also try to walk along a line of bricks or step from one brick to another, so that they practice balancing the weight of the body. Afterwards they should try to explore a mime theme concerned with 'crossing a river' so that they begin to understand how they can put the information they have just gathered to a more imaginative and creative use.

STAGE TWO

Older reception children and six-year-olds should make a more precise exploration of the particular individual modes of locomotion.

Walking

They should be encouraged to adopt a good stance before commencing to walk, to walk freely, swinging the leg from the hip, putting the heel down first and following through with the rest of the foot, pointing the feet directly ahead.

Although it may be felt that controlled exercises may kill some creative spontaneity, in fact they do help some children to be more resourceful during later creative explorations, and they help all the children to gain control of body action.

The exercise should involve:

1 Walking forwards, backwards and sideways, exploring all the space in the room, weaving in, out, between and around the other children.
2 An exploration of the lengths of strides that are possible.
3 Encouragement to listen to the sound of their footsteps, and to explore stamping, walking stealthily and quietly on tiptoes.
4 Varying the height at which they walk and exploring walking on tiptoes, ball of foot, heels, knees, all fours; walking on two hands and one leg, or two legs and one hand, crawling walking on elbows and knees, or on bottom propelled by feet. They should assume crab position and explore crab walking.

5 Practising marking time, thrusting knees upwards to tummy height, stretching ankles and pointing the toes downwards.
6 Working to a percussion or mouthed *sound signal* given by the teacher.

20 *Walking: a simple response to a continuous signal beat*

When the children have become familiar with this kind of work the exercises should involve:

7 Working to a *stop signal*. They should walk about, fitting their steps to the *sound signal* but stop on the *loud stop signal*. It is very important to help children to become aware that a good stop is very important in movement work. Many children are unable to stop suddenly, they overbalance or take another step forward. It is necessary to develop their ability to be able to stop abruptly. Often the children enjoy the activity if they are asked to stop in a 'statue position'. This allows them to use their imagination to adopt an interesting body position.
8 *Phrasing* can be introduced next. Two *sound signals* should be given. One should be staccato, lively and regular for short steps, and the children should explore moving about, altering their gait according to the signals, so that they begin to experience fitting two phrases together.

9 Lastly *pausing*. The children should move to the *step sound signal,* listen for the *stop signal* and stop and pause, standing still, until the *step sound signal* recommences.

Thus they have explored a more controlled movement sequence; *step, step, step, pause, step, step, step, stop*. The introduction of conscious pausing is very important. Young children do not often understand the need for it and it is necessary to help them to see its value by explaining to them that when we are making something and have finished one part, we need a little time to rest and think before we can do the next part, so movement pausing is necessary when one movement or phrase has just finished and another phrase is about to begin. Pausing during locomotion sequences is therefore often a helpful beginning to understanding this concept. It is important that the children should realise that a *pause* is as important as an *action* and that it is just as vital.

The children should now be ready to explore making self invented phrases and to accompany these with sounds made by junk instruments which they have made. Groups should begin to explore a particular sound invented by themselves and to show this to the others. Thus group A might choose to walk slowly, stopping and starting, to a regular beat. Group B might shake their sound containers vigorously and explore lively steps, while Group C might choose to glide about to a sustained constant gong sound.

Occasionally they should be encouraged to explore formation marching patterns, using the sound containers to accompany their steps and keeping in straight lines, shoulder to shoulder. With experience they can explore complicated patterns based on a square and this helps them to become more aware of other people. They are also able to explore advancing and retreating aspects of movement. This work can be further emphasised in partner work, when the children advance and retreat from their partner, emphasising the supposed magnetic pull.

In winter, when snow is on the ground, they should be encouraged to walk behind each other and to try to walk in each other's footsteps. They should notice how the leader does not always keep to a straight path but may travel in an undulating line. They should be led to realise how the weather can alter the mode of walking of a normal adult, how he will walk along with regular steps on a fine day, but will walk slowly another time, leaning forward perhaps as he battles his way against a strong wind. How irregular his footsteps become as he slithers about and has no apparent control over his feet on an icy surface. These details are important factors in characterisation and mention of them here perhaps emphasises how this basic

21 *Walking: follow-the-leader in the snow*

awareness is returned to and deepened throughout the year as the seasons change and permit another aspect or factor which conditions movement to be brought into relevant and purposeful view. The teacher might even arrange her programme to fit in with the seasons. Thus, in spring, she might concentrate on themes concerned with uncurling, opening, growing and link it with nature. Or in autumn, base her themes on twirling and jumping activities, linking them with observation of falling leaves and seeds and spinning or rocketing fireworks in November.

STAGE THREE

Six-year-olds and seven-year-olds should begin to explore different varieties of gait; stride, stalk, strut, plod, shuffle, trudge, tramp, rove, creep, crawl, saunter, jogtrot, stagger, glide, slide, dawdle, loiter, hobble, limp, mince, pace up and down. They are simultaneously increasing their vocabulary as they enjoy the work. They should be asked to observe people outside school, how their younger brother toddles along and how their pets move about.

Often they enjoy the opportunity to incorporate and utilise some of these modes of walking during the exploration of simple nursery rhymes such as *The Grand Old Duke of York,* which allows for marching in procession, marking time and the exploration of different height levels. Or perhaps *Jack and Jill,* which allows for two forms of locomotion, variety of pace, and simple characterisation. Some children enjoy trying to convey mood walking. Two groups might investigate a fairy tale such as *Hansel and Gretel.* The first group explore the reluctant walk to the woods when the stones were dropped, and the return journey, picking up the stones and gaining in confidence, happily accelerating their steps as they near home. While the second group explore the later, more confident walk to the woods while dropping breadcrumbs, changing to the sad unhappy walk back, when they discover the birds have eaten the crumbs and they are tired and lost.

They can be encouraged to explore a teacher invented story, or perhaps one invented by themselves, which permits the exploration of pace, gait, quality, height levels, converging, dispersing, advancing, retreating, balance, etc, so that they are able to put their knowledge to a more imaginative use and at the same time become used to the idea of mime exploration which is a useful introduction to creative dance mime.

The children should be encouraged to watch people very closely and to note peculiar personal habits, how some people always step off the pavement with the left foot; how children often try to avoid walking on the lines in the pavement and how this alters their mode of walking. They should be encouraged to notice how carrying an article can unbalance the body, and be allowed to experiment, walking about carrying a carrier-bag full of heavy books, or large bulky parcels, so that they really begin to understand, through experience, something of the difficulty of hampered walking.

They should be encouraged to watch the actions of mechanical toys, to notice the awkward stilted leg movements of mechanical dolls or the slurring feet, as a robot shuffles along. They should be allowed to make a floppy doll, or a guy or a scarecrow before they explore a theme concerned with *Bonfire Night, Harvest,* or *Toys.* If they make the toy first, they can better visualise some of the types of movement that are possible. Some children do not realise that a guy flops and droops because it has no internal support. Nor do they really know how stiff a scarecrow's limbs really are until they have played with one. Sometimes a child can be encouraged to fasten long sticks to his legs and one across his shoulders, tying his arms to it. Often when they physically experience the difficulty of manoeuvreing legs and arms which cannot bend, they are surprised and the resultant mime work becomes worthwhile.

Running

Running is an exhilirating activity which provides children with an endless amount of physical and emotional satisfaction, and it helps them to release tensions and sudden uncontrolled emotional feelings. Practically, it provides a good form of simple limbering up exercises, for running stimulates the blood flow, muscles and co-ordination of mind and body.

At first the children should explore running awareness activities simply through running freely around, which allows them to enjoy the fun of movement, using mouthed sounds to accompany themselves if they feel inclined and if it is significant to a theme they are exploring, eg various droning noises might be used to accompany the supposed movements of an aeroplane zooming around in the sky, perhaps looping the loop, which allows the children to simultaneously explore rising and swooping actions.

Next the children should explore more controlled exercises, with or without percussion sound signals, for these can be introduced as they progress, in the same way that they were introduced in the walking awareness exercises.

1 The children should run at a steady pace around the room, weaving in and out and around people, travelling in a forward, backward or sideways direction.
2 They should explore slip-steps, varying the lengths of stride.
3 They should run on the spot, varying the height of knee lift, sometimes with very quick quiet steps, keeping the feet near to the floor, sometimes with quiet slow-steps lifting knee to tummy height. They should compare these with running slowly with heavy steps or quickly stamping feet down. Sometimes they should simulate the action of running, bending the knees but keeping feet firmly on ground so that they experience pushing the feet into the floor and thus experience the weight of the body and the strength of the movement.
4 They should explore a variety of pace, sometimes accelerating pace then slowing down again.
5 If possible they should be encouraged to run through the school sand pit to experience difficulty of running as feet sink into soft surface. Also if the children attend swimming lessons they might try running in water.
6 Gradually they should work to two signals which help them to combine running and jumping, thus the signals *Tap, tap, tap, bang, stop* would mean *run, run, run, jump, stop* still on landing. During this time they should explore running and jumping

with bound stop on both feet together, and running and leaping landing on one foot only.

7 They should vary the height at which they run.

8 They should explore hampered running; in a sack or three legged race.

Gradually the teacher should endeavour to help older children to learn to run properly, swinging legs freely from hip, using their arms to help them along.

9 During physical education lessons the older children should:

Run around, dribbling a ball.
Run while bouncing or patting a ball or bowling a hoop.
Run with a partner, pacing him, sometimes throwing a ball to him.
Run with a partner, attempting a tackle in ball games.

All these activities help to make the children more aware of their bodies in relation to another person or object and this is useful training in the relationship awareness.

They might be encouraged to explore something of what they have discovered during a mime concerned with the theme 'Sports' day.

10 The children should also be encouraged to explore varieties of pace, run, trot, gallop, prance, canter, prowl, leaping runs, run and stride, run and jump, bound, scamper, scuttle, spurt, dash, whisk, tearaway, hasten, skim, hurry, fly, rush along, loop.

They should be encouraged to observe how different animals run, kangaroos lollop, rabbits dash, squirrels scamper, monkeys jump, snakes slither.

11 They should also be encouraged to observe how traffic moves and to use the information in a theme concerned with *A Journey*.

12 Similarly they should be encouraged to notice the smooth running action of mechanical toys and engines, eg the piston rod in a toy steam engine.

Their attention should also be drawn to the way in which different people run about, the tottering run of a baby, the slow laboured run of old people, the swift dash of youth and they should notice how their clothes flap about as they run.

All these factors are useful for later mime exploration work.

Twirling

Twirling actions afford children a great deal of pleasure and can often develop out of running actions. When the children are trying to find a further outlet to release emotionally happy feelings they will suddenly change from a sudden spurt of running, to twirl around instead, sometimes keep to a stationary position, sometimes continuing to travel across the open space, until they collapse on the ground and lie there, enjoying the additional sensation of seeing the world still rotating around them until equilibrium is re-established in the ears.

The children should be encouraged to explore twirling activities both as a means of locomotion and as a means of constantly changing body position and body fronts. Exercises should include:

1 Stand upright, arms stretched out to side and twirl around freely on spot, gradually accelerating pace then slowing down, stopping in open body position.

2 Stand upright, arms by side and twirl around and eventually stop in twisted body position. They should note how it is more difficult to keep one's balance, how having the arms outstretched aided balance. They should explore making simple toys that require the addition of extended fins as an aid to balancing.

3 Twirl around on spot but vary height of body

(a) on tip toes with arms stretched above head;

(b) on knees with arms stretched out to side;

(c) crouching down near ground with arms folded together;

(d) lying down, either face downwards or upwards, arms and legs outstretched, spinning around on floor;

(e) crouching down near to floor and to begin to twirl around slowly, gradually increasing speed as they raise body height until they are twirling very quickly with body upright and fully stretched, continuing until they fall down or begin to decrease speed as they sink slowly down to their original position.

4 Twirl around, travelling across room, accelerating or decelerating pace and varying height at which they twirl body.

5 Explore twirling in stationary position, varying height and waving hands up and down in undulating motion so that the movement is consciously felt in the arms.

OBSERVATION

Children should be encouraged to notice different methods of twirling, revolving, whirling, spinning, winding, twining, coiling, swivelling, twisting, spiralling, curling, circulating, screwing, gyrating, pirouetting and whirligig. They should look out for examples of these in nature or in the movements of objects eg falling feathers and leaves, floating and twisting downwards; quick spin of falling sycamore seeds; smoke and steam spiralling and curling upwards into air; behaviour of wire which is unravelling from coil; speed of rotary blades on father's razor; speed of propeller on toy aeroplane; speed of traffic wheels, and of stationary bike's spun wheel; irregular twisting and untwisting action and undulating turning motion of objects on hanging mobile; spin on thrown ball; gyrations of dropped penny; upward tilted spin of shuttlecock; the undulating gyrations of science toy on pivot; the half twists or full rotation of weather cock in sudden wind; screw 'swivel-turn' as a screw is being screwed into position by a screwdriver; upward coiled twist of bean plant and ivy; circular motion of playpark amusement and merry-go-round in amusement park; behaviour of toys, spinning top, paper science toys, windmill.

The children should be encouraged to make a round bottomed wobbly man. Through play they will discover what happens when the wobbly man is knocked off balance, how it rolls about, rocks and rotates. They they should try to imitate some of the types of movement which they have observed. This helps them to make more worthwhile mime investigations – of themes concerned with acrobats, toys, or explorational assymetric dances.

Rolling

Most children enjoy exploring activities which employ rocking and rolling, partly because the motions are pleasurable, and partly because the children become more aware of their own body when it is pressed hard against the floor. The activity is doubly useful because it helps to extend body awareness and also enlarges the children's knowledge of methods of locomotion.

EXERCISES

1 The children should lie down, either on their tummies or backs, with bodies fully extended and should rock gently from side to side using regular swaying motions.
2 They should lie down, bodies fully extended and roll over for some considerable distance.
3 Lie down and lift legs into air, lower legs simultaneously, lift heads into air, alternating in up and down regular motion.
4 Lie down and curl bodies into ball, rock gently from side to side before rolling over, varying speed according to pace given by sound signal.
5 Some children might try to roll head over heels or heels over head.
6 Some may roll over a friend.
They should also explore rolling down slight inclines in playing fields.

OBSERVATION

They should be encouraged to listen to a drum roll and to watch the quick action of the drum sticks; roll marbles around in a container and listen to the sound; watch marbles, which have been dropped, roll along the ground, noting the difference in speed of large or small ones and the way uneven surfaces affect their motion and direction; watch irregular shaped stones roll along an even surface, a roller at work on a road or grass lawn; notice how animals roll about and roll up a snow ball in winter and watch it grow big.

Jumping

Jumping is an activity which gives children a feeling of satisfaction when they are simply exploring elevating themselves off the ground; and affords them a sense of achievement when they are engaged in activities which require them to jump onto or into boxes, jump over an object or friend, or jump down from a height onto the ground. It is necessary to allow them to explore all kinds of jumping activities including jumping along the ground as a means of locomotion, because it fulfils an emotional and functional need and at the same time helps to provide them with some understanding of all the motions and actions involved in different forms of jumping, which they can recall when they are engaged in creative improvisation.

EXERCISES

The children should explore

1 Jumping from one foot and landing on same foot.
2 Jumping from one foot and landing on the other foot, either travelling across floor, or remaining in same spot.
3 Jumping off one foot and landing on two feet, experimenting with height of jump as well as length of jump.
4 Jumping from two feet, landing on one foot, trying not to take additional steps.
5 Jumping from two feet onto two feet. Jumping as high as they can and tucking feet up beneath them.
6 Jumping from a crouched position to see what kind of jumps are possible, jumping as high as they can, thrusting into space.
7 Bunny hops around the room.
8 Stride jumps.
9 Skip jumps, both with and without skipping ropes.
10 Combination of running, jumping and leaping.

11 Jumping backwards, sideways, and forwards and perhaps invent a formation dance sequence and accompany themselves with mouthed sounds.
12 Jumping from varying heights.
13 Jumping over objects, or into large boxes, and older children jumping from one object to another and playing leap-frog.

OBSERVATION

The children should bend down to pat small or large balls near to the ground. Then stand erect and bounce the balls using firm slashing arm movements. They should explore what they have seen in movement.

They should notice how some things bounce and rebound, while others do not.
They should watch children jumping for joy, or in pain, or in fright.
The should observe animals and birds.
Their attention should be drawn to colour, how some seem to leap out while others seem to recede into the pattern.

6 Creative movement

Creative movement provides children with the opportunity to express and explore their responses to inner feelings and their reactions to stimuli from outside their immediate environment. They use both the impressive (arousing emotion) and expressive (responding to feeling) properties of movement. They are required to make and explore their own personal response during which time they devise their own movements, actions and gestures. No two children make an identical response although they are all working simultaneously within a large or small group and all are pursuing a common idea and exploring a common theme.

Some of the principles fundamental to creative movement are mentioned below to help those teachers who may be unfamiliar with the terms.

In *Modern Educational Dance,* Laban says that every movement is conditioned by four elements: space, effort, body and relationships.

1 The space aspect

Every movement takes place in space, either in the kinesphere or in outer general space, during which time it is conditioned by

(a) Level

Movements can be explored at different levels.

High (in space around shoulders, above head).

Medium (in space around body between shoulders and hips).

Low (in space below hips, around legs and down near to floor).

(b) Direction

Movements can travel forwards and backwards (advancing and retreating), upwards and downwards (rising and sinking), sideways (opening and closing; diagonally), or they can be combined.

(c) Movement in relation to the body

Movements may start from centre of body and move outwards from body; around the periphery. They can be narrow, made close to the body, medium-sized and made near to the body; large and travel away from the body; or they may vary between these degrees.

(d) Shape of the movement

We can observe the pattern made by movements as they travel in a pathway through air or along floor. These patterns can be

Straight continuing in an undeviating line.

Curved travelling in a circular pathway which may grow larger or smaller or spiral.

Twisted involving contra directional movements.
Angular involving abrupt changes of direction.

2 Effort
The quality of movement is conditioned by
(*a*) Time element
This refers to the speed of movements, which may be long or short, sudden or sustained, start slowly and accelerate, start quickly and decelerate, or they can be combined.
(*b*) Weight element
This is concerned with muscular tension in body. Some movements are
Firm strong, powerful, held 'gripped', inducing tension in muscles.
Fine delicate light touch, do not induce tension.
(*c*) During movement body position can alter.
It is possible to observe the FLOW of action during changes in body posture. It can be *Successive* action moving from joint to joint successively, eg raising arm hand leads wrist, wrist leads elbow, elbow leads shoulder, thus arm is raised in successive sequence.
Simultaneous action occurs in joints and limbs at same time, whole body part moves as one piece.
Bound action can be stopped and held, gripped at any given point.
These qualities of time, weight, space, can be combined together in eight basic actions; FLICKING, PRESSING, THRUSTING, FLOATING, WRINGING, DABBING, SLASHING, GLIDING.
At the same time movement is conditioned by the body itself.

3 Body
Movement is conditioned by body activity through
(*a*) Locomotion, running, etc.
(*b*) Elevation, jumping, etc.
(*c*) Turning, body fronts are changed when twirling either at one height level, or when spiralling up and down.
(*d*) Rising and sinking when action is concerned with feeling pull of gravity.
(*e*) Opening and closing concerned with stretching body as wide apart as possible, emphasising openness of body (focusing attention out of body) or is concerned with contracting limbs and curling them close, together, (focusing attention inside body).
(*f*) Advancing and retreating concerned with moving forwards, and is stressed as body leans forward, arm reaching out, striving

forward; or is concerned with moving backwards and is stressed as arms are withdrawn and body leans backwards.

(g) Gesture using arms, legs, elbows, feet, knees to penetrate space and shape movements in air or along ground.

22 *The theme of growing*

Body shape

Symmetry of body can be observed when both sides of the body conform exactly in opposite parts and the body is truly balanced.
Asymmetry the body becomes asymmetrical when emphasis is given to one side of the body through gesture, hip dropped, arm lifted and body is unbalanced.
During movement the whole shape of the body alters. It assumes four main shapes; thin, curled up, spread out broad, angular, and twisted.

4 Relationships

The various parts of the body can be related to each other when the body is resting or is active. It can be related to space when attention is focused out of body. It can be related to other people when close together or far apart, during meeting, parting, rising, sinking, advancing, retreating, travelling.

METHOD

Preferably the hall should be used but any unconfined area is suitable. The shape is immaterial; indeed a variety of spacial areas present the children with additional challenges in utilising space. However, if the playing field is used, the children should be made to realise that they cannot explore the whole width and breadth of it, because if they travel too far away, the sound-signals will not be heard.

The children should work in vests and underpants or trousers and should work barefooted, unless parents strongly object.

EQUIPMENT

At first the teacher will probably use self invented mouth sound-signals but gradually she will need tambor, tambourine, drum and gong. More experienced children will need junk sound containers and percussion instruments. Some teachers may prefer to work using records that have specially been prepared for movement work, such as records 1, 2, 3, 4, 5 of the 'Listen and Move series' produced by MacDonald and Evans, Educational Recordings; 6, 7, 8 are not suitable for infants or younger juniors.

Other teachers may prefer to use a piano to stimulate the children's responses and they will find the Listen and Move book series book useful. In later stages the teacher may use tapes prepared by herself.

The work will develop in stages which follow on from one another and are based on eight themes indicated by Laban as being suitable for work with young children.

Theme 1 concerned with body awareness
Theme 2 concerned with awareness of weight and time
Theme 3 concerned with awareness of space
Theme 4 concerned with awareness of the flow and the weight of the body in space
Theme 5 concerned with adaptation to partners
Theme 6 concerned with instrumental use of limbs
Theme 7 concerned with isolated actions
Theme 8 concerned with occupational rhythms

STAGE ONE

The children should work with the teacher to explore activities which involve the 'total stir of the whole being', during exploration of shared movement. The teacher acts as leader and as sound-sign director, using mouthed sounds. The very young children and those who are insecure are happier if they follow her, exploring all the total floor space in the hall and also the air space above their heads, around bodies at medium height and low down near floor. It helps them to feel more secure, both in belonging and working with a group and in their response to the work. Also it tends to quicken their responses to other people. They should explore all the possibilities of locomotion, sometimes travelling on tip toes with body stretched out, hands dancing high in the air; sometimes they should travel bent at medium height or in hunched up position low down, hands dancing on or near floor. They will be concerned with contrasting two main speeds, quick and slow. Sometimes they should travel along circular or straight pathways, exploring unison movement, occasionally pausing between sequences to introduce the idea of phrasing. Occasionally they should stop abruptly on signal and hold body position bound (statue).

Gradually, the teacher should begin to leave the group, retreating (breaking imaginary thread). The children should reach out to her when she reaches new part of room. They should attempt to draw her back. She should resist, then reach out to them, begin to advance slowly towards them, gradually accelerating pace until she rejoins them. When she reaches them they might explore unison investigation of sinking and curling actions, rising and opening movements. Alternatively, sometimes they might work in opposition to her, sinking and curling as she rises, or rise, exploring twisted, broad or elongated thin body shapes, (chin raised as they look at the ceiling, focusing attention on it) while she sinks downwards and curls up, focusing attention on body.

After a period of travelling together as a group, they should stop and pause, the teacher should remain where she is, but the children, as a whole group, should attempt to pull away from her, then return on new signal to gather round her. This introduces the idea of dispersing and converging, advancing and retreating.

STAGE TWO

The teacher should work as sound-signals director, using mouthed and percussion signals. She should gather the children around her in a group, perhaps seated on floor. They should be asked to look at their hands, to open them quickly several times. They should repeat this activity working to drum signal. Then explore opening their hands slowly, working to slow sustained gong signal. Next they should lie down and curl up into ball shape. They should uncurl quickly to drum signal or slowly to gong signal. Then they should explore, responding to various signals which allow them to freely explore rising, twisting, opening, sinking, closing and curling. At the same time they should explore high and low movements, made close to the body, or wide movements made away from the body, responding to various signals, varying speed of movement.

Similarly, they should explore different ways of travelling around room, in a single phrase exploration, responding to different signals, using all forms of locomotion, twirling and elevation, investigating various space levels, varying speed of movement as signals dictate.

23 Spontaneous response to a stoccato beat

As soon as they have become familiar with this kind of work they should explore fitting phrases together. Two signals A and B of contrasting speed, should be played so that the children can think how they will respond. They should practise working to signal A, responding individually within the group. Then they should practise working to signal B. The teacher should explain that they have explored two separate phrases. They must now fit them together, so that they form a movement sequence, A.B.A. They must listen carefully, changing their response as she varies signals, without pausing during the change over from one phrase to the next.

At first the sequences may be concerned with simply linking two locomotion phrases together, then three or four, so that a movement sentence can be explored. Towards the end of the year, when they are familiar with this procedure, they can begin to fit different kinds of movement phrases together, eg (two phrases) running changing to twirling, or (three phrases) begin curled up, change to rising, then to some form of travelling. They must also be led to realise that the procedure can be an add-on exploration, thus, they might commence with simply linking rolling with curling up into a ball. Next, link rolling, curling with rising. Next explore, rolling, curling, rising and twisting. Then rolling, curling, rising, twisting and travelling, until they eventually explore the whole sequence, sink down to floor again and recommence rolling. Thus they have explored a simple creative dance.

At this stage the children should be encouraged to work as sound signals directors, and also occasionally to use sound containers to accompany their movements.

Partner work They should also begin simple partner work. They should explore simple mirror work with a particular partner, rising

24 The beginning of partner work

and sinking, with him or in opposition to him. They should also explore travelling alone and advancing to meet a partner, then retreating from him. Sometimes they can travel together around the room, then separate, travel on alone, advance to meet partner then travel on together.

25 Partner work: sensitivity to partner not yet developed

STAGE THREE

The children will continue to make individual responses within group explorations, continuing similar investigations as previously, travelling in straight, curved and circular pathways, and should begin to explore twisted pathways. Now however stress must be placed on emphasising the use of different parts of body, allowing finger, elbow, knee, foot, chin to lead the child into movement explorations.

Thus, the child may let his finger lead him upwards from curled up position. He must concentrate on it during the process. Sometimes his elbow may lead him downwards. Similarly, his foot might lead him into an exploration along the surface of the floor.

Emphasis must also be placed on the effort aspect, really lifting the knee high, thrusting it into space, really pushing the feet into the ground. Stress should also be placed on quality of touch, bring hands together slowly, fingers touching lightly or clapping hands firmly, noisily, above head when hands dance high. They must really experience holding movements bound and really 'gripped'.

Emphasis must also be laid on more control and precision during partner work. During advancing and retreating, stress must be placed on the 'magnetic pull' or 'magnetic release' of partner. At the same time, partner work should develop into short conversations or question and answer dances or mirror dances. The children can also begin to explore shadow dances when they are travelling.

During this stage, the children should begin to work in two main groups. They can travel round the room in clockwise or anti-clockwise directions, exploring different pathways. One group may explore air space above their heads, while the other group concentrate on space near floor. They can advance and meet each other, one group rising as other group sinks downwards. Similarly during rising, one group may explore opening and spreading movements, while the other group concentrate on small narrow movements. This simple exploration could develop into a group question and answer dance, using mouthed, or sound container, sounds, as an additional refinement.

So far, the children have been concerned mainly with themes based on response to stimuli. Now, they can begin to explore themes based on the action of machinery (clocks, piston rods, wheels), using simple repetitive actions of one part of body to simulate limited mechanical movements, eg sustained circular arm movements simulate wheels beginning to turn slowly, gradually accelerating pace then decelerating slowly until they come to abrupt or slow stop. They may mark-time, thrusting knees high to simulate pumping action of pumping machine. They may swing legs from side to side, with even stretch to simulate clock pendulum. They may use jerky bound actions to simulate movement of piston.

STAGE FOUR

The children will be able to respond individually within the complete group. They should begin to work in several small groups, making several individual group investigations, exploring themes which involve advancing, retreating, opening, closing, rising, sinking, spreading, shrinking, converging, travelling in curved, circular, straight, and twisted pathways, during which they should deepen their capacity to move between speed and height.

Their attention should be drawn to symmetry and asymmetry in the body. The concept of symmetry should be deepened through art work, (they should explore making symmetrical patterns or prints, and make inkblots and obtain a direct symmetrical imprint when the page is folded over; similarly they should make junk toys which depend on symmetry and balance as an integral part of their play value).

Emphasis should be placed on refinement in movement work, ie the precise use of finger, gesture, facial expression. This can be stressed in particular during statue investigation dances, so that they begin to understand the need to move with better precision and clarity of movement. At the same time, their attention should be drawn to basic effort, qualities, slashing, flicking, quivering, punching, thrusting, wringing, tapping, dabbing, floating, gliding, skimming. They should explore themes which involve these basic effort qualities, so that emphasis can be placed on slashing (arms and legs) flicking (hands and feet) punching and thrusting limbs into space, dabbing and tapping (in air, on floor, and around periphery of body) wringing (hands) quivering (hands and feet) floating, gliding and skimming (across surface of floor) or gliding and floating (upwards, when spiralling upwards).

They should also be encouraged to explore using limbs as tools during investigations of themes concerned with smoothing, scooping, scattering, strewing, shovelling, gripping, pinching. They should explore tone and mood in movement, beginning with a percussion stimuli that is quiet, gentle, sustained and use strewing movement of hands and feet and slow sustained travelling hands gliding through air. They should change movements when sound-signal stimulus becomes more dynamic and louder and use lively, quick abrupt actions, that penetrate upwards and downwards and change direction rapidly. Eventually they should be able to explore this form of investigation so that the theme can build up to a climax which ends the exploration.

Similarly, they should explore movements and actions based on primitive work movements, ie, movements essential in the performance of work, chopping, sawing, hammering, sewing, screwing, lifting, smoothing, stitching, cutting, scything, flailing, building, digging, hunting, rolling, dragging (along, from behind, sideways twisting body during process) pulling motions (upwards, downwards, along, or across). Then they should be encouraged to explore themes which allow them to investigate these basic effort qualities, eg theme concerned with agriculture. They could begin with tilling and preparing soil, scatter seeds, explore growth of plant and finally harvest time. They could explore themes based on desert island life, bible stories, fiction, or invent their own fantasy themes.

Lastly they should begin to explore abstract themes based on abstract qualities in movement, syncopated movements, perky movements, lively movements, ponderous movements, rocking movements, rhythmic movements and fine and weighty movements. They could be encouraged to work in different groups and to work out a group response to express one of these qualities which can be incorporated into a class creative dance suite.

26 *Beginning work with percussion instruments. One member of the group controls the beat*

27 *Each child responds to his own percussion sound*

28 *Coordination becomes easier with experience*

7 Mime

The ability to communicate feelings, ideas, desires and responses through non-verbal communication is inherent in man. One has only to watch two children with an apple, to see the degree of communication that is possible. The apple owner eats the fruit with obvious relish, whilst the other child stands by, his body and hands motionless, his eyes watching and concentrating on his friend's activity. His intense longing to bite the apple, is shown through eye and facial expression and is projected and communicated to his friend so intensely that the other child is made to proffer the apple and they share it, bite by bite, with mutual enjoyment. The children have a heightened degree of awareness of each other, the apple and the activity and their elation when the apple is finished, may even invoke further communication of shared happiness through movement. Indeed the two young children observed in the above situation, did in actual fact, fling their arms around each other in a kind of invented hugging dance. Hunger satisfied, humble movement creativity began.

It is on this level of heightened awareness invoking intuitive understanding and creative response that young children should move into detailed expressionist mime involvement.

Discipline problems can arise because many children must remain inactive whilst an individual child or group makes their explorations. They become impatient if they are anxious to make their own investigations. The children should be led to realise that the teacher will allow them all to make an exploration as soon as possible and that a theme can be explored for several days if necessary. They will not become bored if this happens, because they then approach the theme from a variety of different angles. For instance, if the theme is *Mother*, some children may make an investigation of mother engaged in different household tasks, others may explore mother as a friend who plays with them and the baby. Therefore a variety of facial expression, gestures, movements and incidents are catered for, which holds the children's interest in the theme and at the same time enlarges their total conception of the theme *Mother*.

Although many children are willing to suggest themes which they would like to explore, eg getting up in the morning, their first investigations are generally poor because they have only a hazy understanding of the movements connected with the activity they are trying to describe. Consequently, it is useful if the teacher-controlled involvement in mime is a direct follow up of an immediate

observed incident, so that the children's attention can be drawn to the types of movement used during a particular activity.
Method

Stage 1 Individual response based on direct observation

The class should work as a whole group. An area should be cleared so that there is space for the children to sit on the floor, grouped in a semi-circle, leaving space directly in front of the teacher. A child should be asked to perform a simple task using props, ie fetch a chair and sit down on it, choose a book from the library corner or pick up a skipping rope and skip. The other children should watch child A. When he has finished, a volunteer should be asked to mime the incident he has just witnessed. When child B has finished, the children should be asked to comment on his interpretation. Often, the children in the audience will remember certain movements made by child A which child B had forgotten to include in his interpretation. Then child C who has remembered them should be asked to make his exploration. Further discussion about his portrayal should be encouraged. In this way the involvement is deepened and becomes a meaningful activity. The follow-up discussion should also lead the children to consider basic questions concerning movement and gesture. Do all people skip with both feet together or do some begin with the left foot? Other children should be asked to perform the original task so that the children have a variety of observed incidents on which to base their opinions and interpretations.

Stage 2 Individual response based on remembered observation

Gradually, as the children progress and begin to acquire a store of remembered incidents, the need for the actual performance of a simple task in front of them lessens. Many children become able to base their work entirely on memory. Individual children can be asked to volunteer to make an exploration concerned with simple actions, washing themselves, cleaning their teeth, eating a banana, blowing up a balloon, drinking a cup of hot milk. After their investigations are finished, the mimes should be discussed and the children should be asked to comment on the aptness of the facial expressions and gestures made by the performers. The best mimes might be repeated and perhaps put into a little sequence, thus a child might mime eating a banana, drink his hot milk, and then clean his teeth, so that the children begin to see how to work out simple story themes for mime.

Themes based on domestic situations present ample opportunity for varying investigations during which it is possible to begin to deepen the children's awareness of how all kinds of incidents finally combine together to make up a total process such as washing themselves. For instance, during a first investigation, a child might only make arbitrary dabbing movements. After discussion, he can be led to remember to put the plug in the sink before he turns on the tap, to pick up the soap and to wet his sponge before he washes himself. Next, an even deeper awareness of the process of washing can be developed and he can include such refinements as opening the bathroom door, switching the light on, undressing, testing the water after it has run into the bowl, lathering the sponge, rubbing the lather onto his neck and ears as well as his face, rinsing thoroughly, reaching for towel to dry himself, replacing it on peg after use, pulling out plug, switching off light, opening and closing door as he leaves the bathroom. These are little incidentals which form part of the total process of washing which the children must be encouraged to notice and include in their interpretations as they grow in ability through practice and experience.

Often, an awareness of the process of dressing can be developed more quickly, if the children are involved in a mime investigation following directly on from a physical education lesson. Their previous struggles while dressing themselves (to turn a garment right side out, fasten a button at shoulder level, tie a bow behind their backs) are still fresh in the mind and are incidents which add interest to an investigation of the process of dressing.

The children should be encouraged to compile a scrap book of incidents which emphasise simple daily tasks. At its simplest, it could be a collection of pictures cut from magazines which depict the family at home, father shaving, mother cooking, grand-mother visiting, baby eating food etc, which they could glance through to refresh their memory before making a mime exploration.

Insecure children however still feel the need to base their work on direct observation. If the opportunity occurs that the school gardener can be observed at work, the children should be allowed to go to the window to watch him for a few minutes. Then, they should return to the open space area and all the children should be encouraged to explore some of the movements they have seen him perform such as walking, digging, weeding, planting, resting on his shovel. Then volunteers should be asked to come forward to make a mime interpretation of some other gardeners, perhaps park gardeners, or people engaged in gardening activities whom they have previously observed. A theme about gardening should be discussed and the children should be allowed to make a simple group exploration based on the theme, a garden. The individual child will be concerned with exploring only his own particular aspect of gardening while working simultaneously with the group. So the total exploration could involve simultaneously, father cutting the hedge, big brother mowing the lawn, mother weeding, baby crawling on the grass and themselves helping to trundle a wheelbarrow.

At this stage it is also essential to draw the children's attention to occupational activities and to make them aware how particular activities condition the type of movements, action, gestures and facial expressions which a person will make while engaged in an activity. They should be encouraged to notice incidents that are conditioned by the use of tools, ie mending a puncture, baking a cake, which they can later explore in mime. Thus, they might be encouraged to go home and watch mother engaged in a domestic chore. Often it is possible to use their subsequent interpretations to make a comparison of the different use of whole body movements and smaller precise actions when a person is engaged in a particular activity. Thus, if the theme is sewing, child A might base his exploration of mother working a treadle machine. She must be seated, so her whole body movements can include, bending, swaying, rocking, twisting and turning, while finer actions will include precise arm, hand and finger actions. Her knees and legs must move up and down, her feet pat or shuffle between rests while she turns the garments. Child B, might base his exploration on mother sewing by hand. She may have similar whole body movements, but her hand, feet and leg actions will be entirely different. Thus the children can be led to consider several aspects of a simple activity such as sewing, and they begin to realise that a theme can be interpretated in many ways, not simply the first obvious way. That careful thought is needed before they begin a mime.

These early mime investigations are in reality the beginning of co-ordinated commentaries and descriptions. It is now necessary to emphasise the need for a better awareness of precise facial expression, which helps to refine a mime interpretation. The work can follow closely on from direct observation at the centres of interest concerned with sense awareness discovery.

Stage 3 Facial expression

The children can work simultaneously as a whole class. Preferably they should sit on the floor, in a semi-circle, close to the teacher. Each child will make his individual response, within the group, to a teacher directed suggestion. The teacher should discuss with the children the kind of incidents which might cause a person's facial expression to change, sudden fright, shock, pain, good news, sympathy, reactions to heat, cold, smells. Next the children can make individual responses, in a round-robin-fashion to suggestions called out quickly; joy, fear, anger, mischief, toothache, etc, so each child is exploring a different theme and cannot copy his neighbour's thoughts and responses. It is necessary that the children work quickly at first so the themes must be suggested cracker-jack fashion, this helps the children to think quickly, react quickly and make a speedy response. A few volunteers might come to the front of the class to show their ideas. Then the children themselves can be asked to think of a theme to which they can respond.

After the involvement, the teacher might try to encourage the class to think and discuss how they might express these reactions or feelings in words. After one such lesson, where the theme explored had been *Happiness,* a five-year old girl said 'Happiness is a piece of sunshine shining on the grass'. Later she painted a picture to emphasise her statement. In another class, a seven year old boy remarked 'When I am happy, I feel like a little twinkling star'. Asked what he felt like when he was unhappy. He replied, 'Burnt toast'. Thus the mime lesson can be closely linked with the development of an awareness of language and could lead the children to discover how poets use images to describe their feelings, eg in *Crash Car Blues* by Adrian Henri, he writes:

You make me feel like
a used *Elastoplast.*

When the children have become familiar with these simple facial responses, they can also learn to make a duo-exploration, that is one child investigates two parts, eg mother and daughter. The child is required to make her first response (perhaps a child in pain) then she must mime her mother's reaction to seeing the child in pain. The two reactions must follow on each other. The length of time which the expression is held can be determined by a gong-signal sound. The child is told the theme, the gong is struck and the child responds, mimes and holds the expression until the signal fades away, on the second gong signal she responds to the second part of the theme. This helps them to understand the value of 'time' in mime.

29-36 FACIAL RESPONSES

29 Happiness

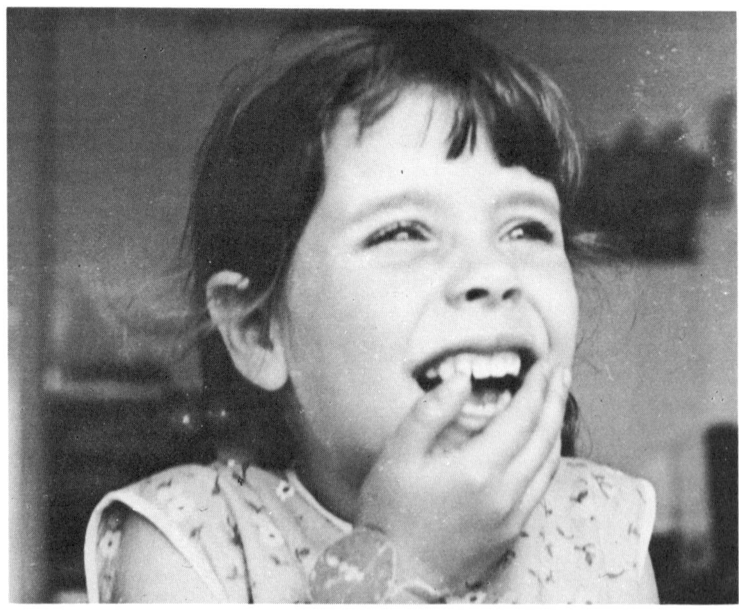

30 Mischief

31 *Toothache*

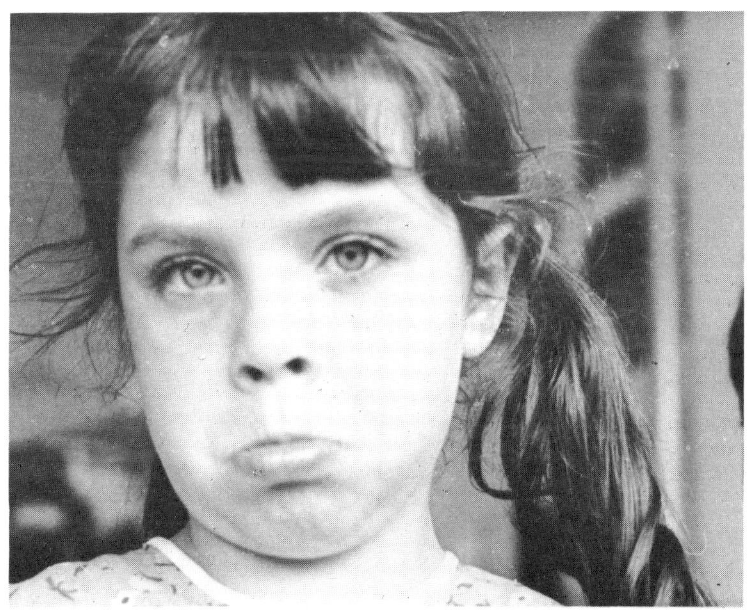

32 *Petulance*

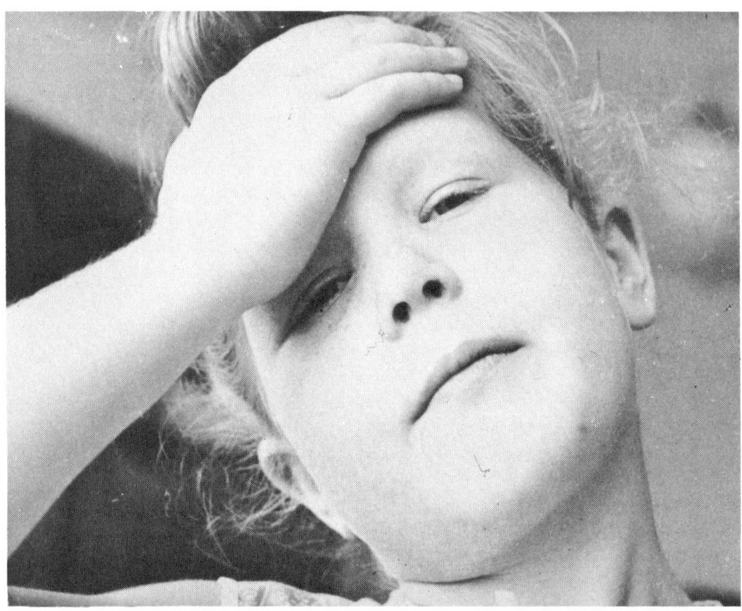

33 *Frustration*

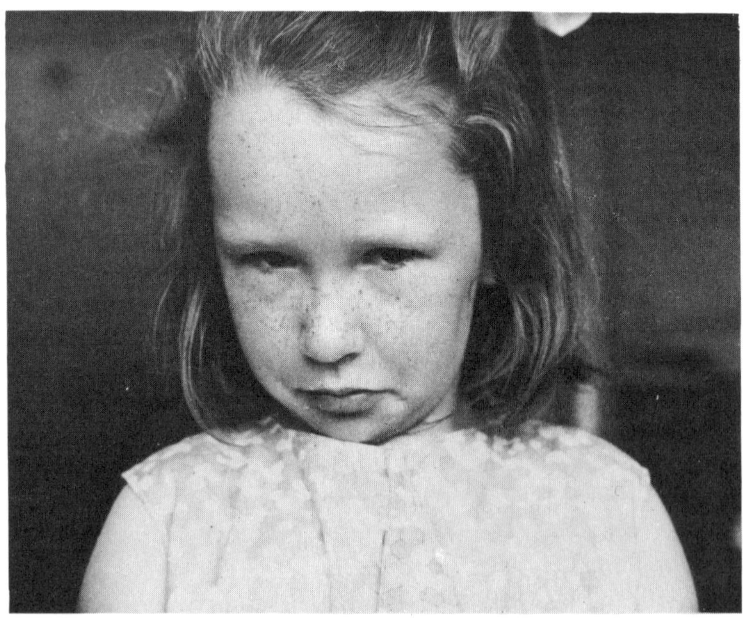

34 *Displeasure*

35 *After a fist blow – purely mime*

36 *Pretending to be teacher who is cross with her class*

Stage 4 Partner work

The children should now be ready to work in very close co-operation with a partner exploring a theme concerned with mirror work. One child is supposed to be herself looking in a mirror. The other child is the reflection. The two children should face each other. They must observe each other very deeply. The second child must copy the exact facial expressions and hand movements of the other child. As they become used to this work, they can pretend that the mirror is full length, which permits them to include walking backwards away from the mirror, half turning to see their full length reflection, useful for themes concerned with dressing.

37 Excellent mirror work by Sandra and Shirley

In fact, the children can incorporate the exercise into a theme which is controlled by a 'situation-site', for instance, in a dress shop. The shopper, is undressed standing in a cubicle, her movements can only include dressing, undressing, viewing her reflection, showing her responses to it and also to her first impressions of garments handed to her by the shop assistant. The saleswoman, will move about fetching and carrying so her movements will include, elevation, locomotion as well as facial expression.

These themes controlled by a 'situation-site' help the children to tighten up their thoughts and to use their imagination. They need to think more deeply about how they can convey the maximum information when they are so tightly controlled by the limited situation-site. It is often easier if they begin to explore this kind of theme through using a situation with which they are completely familiar such as a garden wall. One group may decide to explore it as a wall which they can approach, peep through and climb over. Another group may explore an actual situation they may have observed, such as two neighbours talking over the wall. The mine will be conditioned by the supposed height of the wall. They are forced to use their imagination and ingenuity to evolve a theme which will allow for plenty of movement and facial response.

Some children enjoy trying to interpretate a situation-site mime basing their improvisation on nursery rhymes such as *Little Miss Muffet*.

Stage 5 Imaginative characterisation

So far, the children have been exploring incidents which are more or less based on fact. Now it is necessary to help them to explore inventing a personality for their character.

At first, some children enjoy trying to interpret a scene they have observed on television, perhaps based on cowboys. The main incidents follow closely on what they have seen, but their interpretation of the cowboys' characters can be entirely different. Girls often like to explore fairy tale cartoon characters which they have watched. Often, however, their interpretations are coloured by a stereotyped conception of a queen or stepmother formed and conditioned by the original cartoon. It is necessary to help them to realise that all stepmothers are not cruel as was Hansel and Gretel's, nor witches like Snow White's, so that they are better able to make their own imaginative interpretation of a fairy tale or imagined character.

The children should also begin to explore working out a personality for different characters from literature, so that they can begin to explore simple imaginative stories such as *Whistle for Willie* by Ezra Jack Keats (Penguin Books). This is a simple tale about a boy who cannot whistle but who learns to do so. There is ample opportunity for characterisation, locomotion, elevation, balance, mood, and facial expression.

A group of children often enjoy exploring *Barnabas-Ball* by Robin and Inge Hyman, published by Evans Brothers. They can enjoy looking at the colourful illustrations and generally they feel extremely sympathetic to the animals in the story. The children can explore the simple story and then can be encouraged to invent a similar simple story concerned with a zoo. The story is also useful as a first exploration of a printed script in verbal drama exercises for more experienced children.

Their imagination can be given full outlet in an exploration of the story *Where The Wild Things Are* by Maurice Sendak, published by Bodley Head. This is a tale of fantasy, about a boy who is dreaming about an island full of wild animals. This story is particularly useful as it can be used in several ways. It can be explored firstly during story time, when the children (while seated around the teacher) can be encouraged to mime the animals and explore roaring, growling etc. Secondly, it can be explored more fully as a simple mime. After space has been cleared to allow the children to roam about freely, they can explore 'the island', utilising and exaggerating all their previous observed knowledge of wild life to invent truly imaginative animals.

38 The men left the island and the women huddle together for protection and to decide what to do

39 The women do the housework

40 They look for the return of the boat

41 The boat returns

42 The men tell of their adventures

43 A party is given to celebrate their safe return

38–43 THE ISLAND

38

39

40

41

42

43

Thirdly, it can be used to introduce children to creative dance explorations. During which, one group of children can explore the imaginary forest which grows during the night, another group can explore the animals, another group the movement of the sea over which the boy sails to the island, and one child can explore being the child. Often, it leads children on to invent their own fantasy themes.

Some children are happier if they base their mimes on true facts such as incidents from history or stories from the Bible. They are happy to make larger group explorations especially if they are allowed to use clothes from the dressing up box or to make impromptu costumes using lengths of material from the touch awareness table. Often they unconsciously begin to break into speech during these explorations as they become carried away with portraying the character and this leads them quite naturally into verbal drama, and they may begin again making a re-exploration of the immediate theme.

44–46 THE STORY OF MOSES

44 Moses tells the people to follow him and he will lead them to safety

45 *They follow him*

46 *The people are led to freedom and Moses is exultant*

8 Verbal drama improvisations

Stage 1 First year

Young children should be led gradually towards verbal drama improvisations. A great deal of time will be spent on story participation, which helps the children to overcome shyness and encourages them to begin to work together without quarrelling. It develops a feeling for literature and enlarges their repertoire of stories and at the same time helps them to appreciate the dramatic elements in literature. A great deal of work will also be concerned with body awareness, sense discovery and sound awareness activities, which provide a basis for discussions. Periods of talking together and discussing the stories they have heard, helps to start the children talking and thinking. Further periods of talking to the teacher in whole class involvements should help them to enjoy communicating with others and perhaps enjoy airing freely their views and opinions. They may even become keen to come forward to the front of the class to address the audience, while they tell the class about something which has interested them – some incident they have witnessed or something that has already happened to them, or is going to happen (eg being a bridesmaid). The children are being encouraged all the time to think, to describe and to illustrate their ideas through use of words. They are thus using their immediate vocabulary and are adding new words to it, as they hear unknown words used by other children during their descriptions of incidents.

In the reception class most of the creative drama work will be concerned with poetry and movement work and with mime and sound stories invented by the children and explored in class participation activities. Occasionally some children may be encouraged to explore simple nursery rhymes such as *Goldilocks, Sing a Song of Sixpence* or *Simple Simon.*

During Wendy House play, the children will automatically and unknowingly begin to explore simple free drama, mainly themes based on home life. They should be encouraged to think up an event which they can include in a play, eg put on outdoor clothes and take the baby for a walk in the park and return home again, so that by the second half of the summer term they become able to control and condition Wendy House play from its inception and not simply rely on the play to develop shape and end itself. (This will be useful later, when more controlled verbal improvisation work begins usually in the autumn term of the second year.)

Work with very simple junk puppets will also encourage the children to think aloud and learn to develop and sustain a conversation with a puppet. Even very young children can manage to make a simple puppet out of vegetables, paper tissues and junk materials. The children respond immediately to their creation, for the appeal of puppets is universal. Almost immediately the puppet seems to assume a personality and life of its own. The children readily identify with them, and are happy to sit down and watch an impromptu show, however simply performed. There is no need even for a proper puppet theatre. A curtain stretched between two chairs or a table top over which the puppet can appear will suffice. The children are quite content to watch the teacher or a friend, manipulate and talk to one or two puppets. Their imagination and sympathy is quickly stirred. Although they may be inhibited when talking to teacher they have absolutely no inhibitions in talking back to the puppet if it suddenly leans forward and asks them a question. Shy children can become 'engaged in open conversation' without realising that they are talking freely. Equally, they will happily accompany the puppet in the singing of a song or the recitation of a nonsense rhyme or jingle. Often this is useful in helping self conscious children to join in song although they may not do so in a singing lesson.

At first the children will be happy to work in the simple relationship of child talking to his own particular puppet. Gradually as they become experienced and move towards stage two work, a small group can work together, one child performing and the others listening, taking it in turns. The children learn to develop a conversation, using one voice to represent themselves and one voice for the puppet, during which time they practice the development of a sustained logical conversation or argument, as they fit answers to questions. This forces the children to order their thoughts and tighten up their means of verbal expression. At the same time, they are required to invent a suitable voice to suit the personality of their puppet characters. They are forced to explore the invention of other voices for different kinds of characters, which helps to make the children aware of pitch in oral speech and more aware of the use of the voice as a means of helping characterization. This is a useful introduction to understanding that the voice is a valuable element in the portrayal of any character during ordinary verbal drama explorations.

Sometimes a child is too self-conscious to speak out freely in front of other children and is hesitant to join in an ordinary verbal drama investigation. Often he will speak happily and freely and unselfconsciously when using an invented voice to speak and answer for a puppet, especially if he can kneel down behind the curtain and hide himself away from the audience's view. If he is encouraged to stand up and reveal himself to the audience when the play is finished, he can become used to facing an audience or group of children and so lose his fear of an audience.

Work with puppets can also help the children to try to think more precisely, if the investigation is carried out as part speech, part mime. The child asks the puppet various questions and the puppet answers with gestures, not words. Junk puppets have only a limited amount of actions which they can perform easily. The child needs to become aware of the type of actions which it is possible for his puppet to make, because they will determine the type of question which he can ask the puppet during this kind of investigation. Unless the child is aware of his puppet's limited action capacity he will be hampered in formulating and developing his conversation. At the same time he must realise the limited action capacity determines the way he must learn to handle the puppet otherwise he will be disappointed that his puppet does not seem to work as well as other people's. He must be allowed time simply to practise manipulating a variety of junk and glove puppets, simply to find out the different ways they can be manipulated.

Then the children will be ready to join in a puppet play, wherein the puppets are the actors on stage and they themselves do not appear on stage.

47 *Neil takes a peep at the audience*

48 Sandra and Stephen working their puppets, keep well out of sight

Stage 2 Verbal exploration

As soon as the children have realised that speaking and communicating with others can become an enjoyable and valuable activity, they are ready to begin more controlled verbal explorations during free choice activity time. The children will still be exploring the work on a very elementary level. It is desirable that all children who wish to take part in an improvisation be allowed to do so. If there are forty children in the class this would seem to be a formidable task. Often, however, some children are somewhat hesitant to join in at first, so a class soon sorts itself out into those who are extremely eager, those who are willing to try occasionally, and those who must be gradually coaxed into this kind of activity. They should be encouraged to work in a different part of the room, away from the Wendy House enabling another group to play in the Wendy House while this particular group work in a different corner with the teacher. They are now engaged in 'drama activities', not Wendy House activities. It is necessary to provide a flexible situation, wherein a number of children can explore and re-explore the same theme. Verbal improvisations are therefore better described as 'spontaneous investigations and variations' around themes, which are meaningful to a particular child, according to his environmental and cultural background. It is essential that he begins to explore them with the friends with whom he normally plays, as their vocabulary will be similar to his own. Within an average class, children's vocabulary can vary enormously and some children are unable to understand children from more cultured homes.

The themes must initially be within the natural experience of the children who are taking part, and the children must be allowed to develop the theme according to their own experience of life, although during the discussion which precedes the investigation, the teacher will ask the children to suggest several themes which they would like to explore. Then when they have unanimously agreed on one, perhaps *The Park* the teacher should ask, Which Park? Which particular part of the park? The natural wooded part, play area, swing park, flower and rock garden area, tennis and bowling fields, duckpond? Then she should ask what the children would expect to find in the area. What could they do there? Who might they expect to see? What kind of people? How many? How old? Why might these people be there? What might they be doing? Are there any animals, pets or wild life? What time of the day or night is it? What is the weather like? What time of year? How does the time of day affect what they might expect to happen in the park? What sound might they hear which could influence the plot?

49–52 WENDY HOUSE PLAY

49

50

51

52

49 *Mother and father have breakfast*

50 *Father goes to work*

51 *Mother puts the children to bed*

52 *Tracy, Christine and Deborah tucked up for the night*

Although this may seem to be too logical an approach, it is necessary so that a sense of order and progression can develop during their exploration. It helps the children to begin to think about a park which they have previously visited and they conjure it up in their minds and so have a clearer picture from which to work. Often they will remember incidents which occurred during their visits which can be incorporated in their improvisation and which may provide a starting point for their work. At this stage the level of conversation will still be little more than Wendy House chatter. Indeed, it is most important that the improvisations should arise out of the spontaneous and individual vocabulary of the children, including colloquialisms (and child-invented funny words if they arise, because some children have inadequate vocabulary).

At first the teacher will stay with the children as they struggle to work out their ideas and find words to express what they are trying to say. The teacher may arrange that she will come to tea, and thus will be able to stay awhile and see how the play is developing without inhibiting the children. When they have become used to this kind of work, she may leave the group, to attend to another group, while the children make a few preliminary explorations, and return from time to time to see how they are progressing. Then when the children are satisfied with their work, she will return to watch the whole improvisation straight through, after which she should lead them into a discussion of the work, to find out which bits they think were successful, how they think something might have been improved, etc.

Often already known playground jingles and singing games can be used during verbal explorations. Indeed the playground jingle *Cherry-pie,* led one group of children to make a group verbal improvisation. They had had a considerable amount of previous participation in free Wendy House drama and mime explorations and had begun to explore more controlled verbal improvisations but they had not worked together before as a group.

Although their playlet was little more than a verbal scribbling because their vocabulary was limited, and colloquial, the interest which these children showed, both as actors and audience was deep and intense and was sustained throughout the entire performance, and shows that with practice, drama can become an absorbing, stimulating and rewarding experience for children.

Occasionally the children should show their work to another group and the other group should be asked to comment, and perhaps some children may volunteer to show how they would have acted a certain part. Or a group may make their own investigation which can be shown in the original group.

The children do not waste time and often become very deeply involved in the investigations. Once this stage has been reached it is useful to pursue a slightly more controlled form of investigation.

Stage 3   Second year
METHOD

Preparation for whole class involvement (or group work). The area in which the children are to work must be cleared. Furniture must be stacked so that as large a space as possible is made available, it may be circular or it may be centred to one side of the room. The children can sit on chairs, if the method of working is 'in the round' or on floor if the working space is more suitable to auditorium-type workout.

A child is then asked to volunteer to make a solo verbal improvisation.

The child should be asked to think of a situation in which he could be by himself, and talk to himself or to an invisible person eg a one-sided telephone conversation; reading, cooking or knitting instructions as he works; reading a letter; recording a speech on tape recorder – or slowly singing to himself . . . for own amusement; giving instructions . . . how to make something on TV; writing an article. The child is then asked to mime and make his verbal exploration. The value of a simple mime investigation, just prior to the verbal exploration, is that it helps to conjure up a vivid mental picture in the child's mind of the situation or character in which he is interested. The subsequent verbal exploration enlarges on this mime statement.

The child may also use a doll (baby) and perform functional actions and indulge in play talk, as he baths the baby etc. The other children should be asked to say how they would have extended or altered this performance in discussion time. Then another child should make his investigation.

Developing on from the simple exploration with child and doll or puppet basis, the children work out simple themes which involve

(a) Two children.
Two people engaged in telephone conversation or two people talking together.
Mother and young child.
Mother and older child.
Father and son, mending a puncture.
Child visiting a friend's house.
Mother getting child up in morning.

(b) A person and an animal or pet bird, etc. This allows for verbal communication on the one hand and sensitive miming on the other.

The value of this work is that the children are not just engaged in fun playlets which may be shown to an audience if 'good' enough, they are engaged in working out a theme subject for immediate viewing by an audience. Therefore elements concerned with production now have definitely to be considered more deeply.

(a) Voice production and projection.

(b) The value of timing word and action.

(c) The value of keeping fairly still whilst other person speaks or mimes.

(d) The value of a facial gesture indicating an answer to a spoken comment or order (raised eyebrows, pursed lips, nose screwed up in derision).

(e) Learning how to sustain a conversation for some considerable time (in the free spontaneous investigations, many children can join in and appear to be making valued contributions, to the playlet investigations, yet their conversation may be limited to repeated yes or no statement) – this is clearly shown up in the more controlled explorations – and the child is forced to think more deeply and quickly.

(f) Learning not to hog the limelight. Discipline problems begin to arise because the children in the audience, who are not used to the kind of involvement, quickly tire when they are not active participants. It is necessary therefore that throughout the term, the children should be gradually helped to become a good audience.

53 Amanda and Shama communicate by improvised telephone; such an exercise helps to speed verbal response

In these more controlled kind of investigations, it has been found that many children can begin a conversation, but they can rarely think quickly enough to keep it going. Unnecessary pauses arise because they are still wondering what to say next. Frequent participation with home-made telephones is useful in aiding the children to overcome this. Equally, some children have difficulty in starting a conversation, so explorations using already learnt conversational poems are sometimes helpful. Traditional poems such as *What's your name?* and *Gossip* can help children learn how to develop a duo conversation. Afterwards they can try to make up a similar simple conversation which can be used in their verbal investigations and which can be written down into the class book of recorded creative poetry.

What's your name?

What's your name,
Mary Jane,
Where do you live?
Down the lane,
What do you keep?
A little shop,
What do you sell?
Ginger pop,
How many bottles do you sell in a day?
Twenty four. Now go away.

Gossip

How do you do, neighbour,
Good neighbour, how do you do,
Very well I thank you,
And how is cousin Sue,
Cousin Sue is very well,
And sends her love to you,
And so does cousin Belle,
And how pray, does she do?

Similarly, the poem *There's a hole in my bucket* allows the children to explore characterisation and attempt dialect and they can see how a long conversation can be developed about a very simple theme.

The children also need help in learning to fit action to a sudden command. The simple exercise of mother getting a child up in the morning, for instance, is an excellent theme. The child or children lie on the floor, mother enters the room (having previously left classroom) and wakens them and tells them to get up. It sounds an easy theme, yet many children find it extremely difficult to work out in a convincing way unless they have had plenty of previous mime involvement. For instance, one new class inexperienced in this kind of work tried this exercise without much success. The 'mother' said 'get up', as a simple statement without any element of command in her voice. At first the sleepers awoke and got off the floor just as though they had only been sitting on it. This happened several times, although different children investigated being 'mother'. The teacher discussed with the children how they woke up at home. During the work out one boy managed to think of rubbing his eyes, as though he was still sleepy, but he got out of bed as though he had been sitting on a chair. After further discussion another child thought of sticking his toes out to see if the room was cold – but still the investigations were not developing properly and the children did not seem able to discover for themselves why the investigations were not working. Suddenly a member of the audience asked if she might try. She said she must leave the room and was going to explore being her father getting her mother up. She seemed to wait outside the door a long time and the teacher was just going to look for her when suddenly she burst in, throwing the door back so that it banged on the cupboard behind and shouted loudly, 'Will you get up before I knock your flipping block off'. The voice was loud, forceful and commanding. The child sleeper leapt up, said 'yes sir' and without thinking began to take his pyjamas off hurriedly and to put his clothes on so that he would be ready quickly. The actions were prompt and appropriate and unexpected by both children. The audience burst out laughing. Everyone was delighted. The theme had worked well at last.

Sometimes it becomes necessary to help the children to think more deeply about simple situations. They are adept at thinking of certain actions which they might perform on the level of their own past experience, but do not yet possess the imagination to think up something more unusual. It is helpful therefore if the teacher can at the end of the explorations (or at some other time during the day having made reference to their previous exploration) read a story or poem or extract which might enlarge their vision of what could be encompassed in certain situations, eg if the children have been concerned with exploring the theme *A child visiting another house*, the following extract might serve to provide them with an imaginative idea for a future development.

Extract is from *My Naughty Little Sister is a Curly Girl* by Dorothy Edwards.

> One day, when Winnie and her mother were spending the afternoon at our house, my sister sat staring very hard at

> Winnie's ringlets, and all of a sudden she got up and went over to her and pushed one of her little fingers into Winnie's tidy ringlets.
> Then, because the ringlet looked so nice on her finger, she pushed another finger into another ringlet.
> Now if anyone had interfered with my sister's hair she would have screamed and screamed – she even made a fuss when our mother brushed it – but Winnie sat still and quiet in her mousy way – although I don't think she liked having her hair meddled with any more than my sister would have done.

It is the sort of incident which adds authenticity to a characterisation or exploration and once young children have become aware that this kind of incident should be noticed, they seem to naturally become more aware of such simple incidents and frequently will report such interesting occurrences. It is necessary for the children therefore, that the teacher collates a book of extracts for herself which she can use to widen the children's outlook.

Stage 4 Group work with 4 to 8 children

As soon as the children have become quite familiar with what kind of elements really do contribute towards making an exploration worthwhile, they are ready to re-explore themes which require the participation of seven or eight children, eg themes concerned with launderette or perhaps school. It is essential that the theme has a central point, perhaps the room in the launderette or one particular room in the house. People enter and leave the room, or speak through a window but the theme is controlled by its fixed situation. The children can become extremely involved in this kind of exploration, and there is ample scope for the children to invent incidents, eg *The Clinic* is a theme which allows for a variety of responses and the children can become more involved with the activity as it progresses.

The children might explore the hospital clinic, the dental clinic, or the after-care maternity baby care clinic, (for many children accompany their mother and baby sister or brother in these visits). A group of six year olds explored this theme. It was the first time a larger group exploration had taken place. At first they were rather giggly and silly. Gradually as they became interested they became more deeply involved with the conversation – as the pictures show.

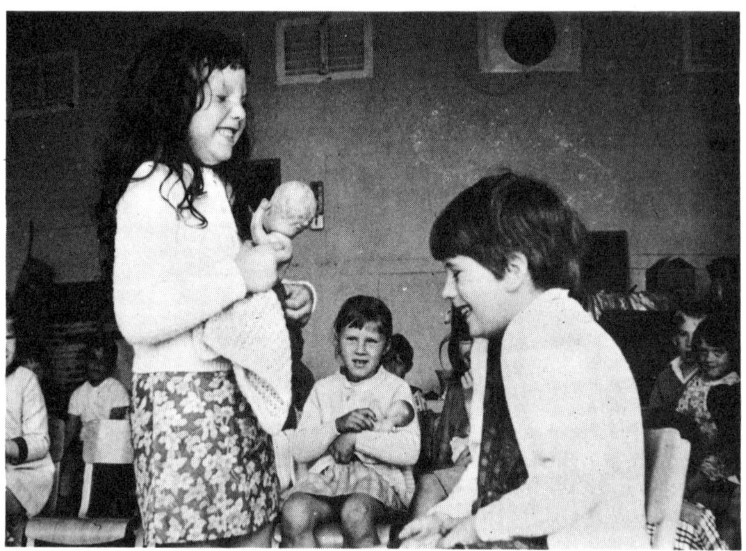

54 The initial embarrassment for such a theme causes Carol and Anne to have the giggles

54–57 THE CLINIC

55 They begin to calm down but Anne still has to bite her tongue

56 *A keen interest in the situation begins to develop*

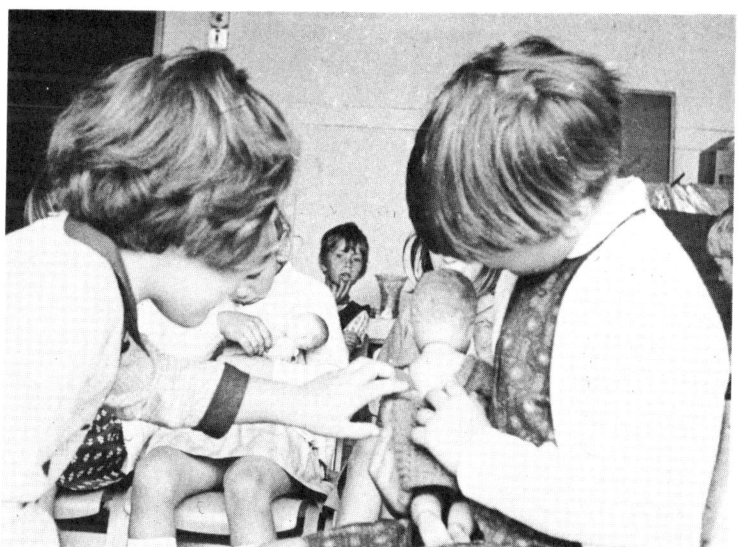

57 *The serious business of doctor examining patient*

Sometimes a theme seems to hang fire, perhaps because the children or one of the children cannot adequately visualise the situation. They are unable to become the character they are trying to investigate. Yet they may succeed admirably when working with a different theme, where their imagination is fired and stimulated by the particular theme, or is one with which they are more personally familiar. In the following photographs, one child who generally succeeds well in plays based on domestic themes, did not enjoy exploring the theme school. She gave up quickly and another child took over. At first she copied the ideas of the first girl, then gradually as she grew more interested, thought up ideas for herself and captured the interest of the other children who were watching, so that they gathered around her to listen to the story she was inventing for the 'class' to hear.

Often when four or five children are working together in a verbal improvisation, the level of the conversation involvement is uneven, one or two children talk freely and continually without meaning to hog the conversation until it develops into a duo conversation simply because the other children do not seem to know how to turn the conversation to include themselves. Simple exploration of poems such as Fire! Fire! Mrs Dyer, can often help them to see how they might use one or two words and be able to make a pertinent statement which continues and develops the conversation.

It must be emphasised that the children are not constantly using the actual words of the poetry as a script. This would be inhibiting. Occasionally however, conversational poems can help the older children who find starting a conversation difficult, to see how they can form a simple and very pertinent conversation.

> Fire! Fire! said Mrs Dyer
> Where! Where! said Mrs Dare
> Up the town! said Mrs Brown
> Any damage! said Mrs Gamage
> None at all! said Mrs Hall

The children could perhaps invent simpler short precise phrases or statements about an incident etc.

Sometimes improvisations can derive out of poetry stimulus. The children might take a narrative verse or complete poem and invent an improvisation based on the idea of the theme, or they might invent a theme which represents the opposite viewpoint of an idea. Sometimes the children are able to develop a theme which derives from 'bits of dialogue' which they may have overheard, eg odd sentences heard when travelling on a bus. They do not know the beginning or the end of the conversation, but they can think up a conversation based on what they think it might have been about. They may not remember and use the exact words in their improvisations but their exploration can derive from the overheard dialogue stimulus. A six year old girl reported seeing a man run out of a shop shouting 'I'll never come in here again!' The sentence formed an interesting topic for discussion, and many reasons were thought up which could explain the incident, and which could be explored in verbal improvisations.

Stage 5 Themes

When the children have become sufficiently experienced and can maintain an investigation of reasonable duration (fifteen to twenty minutes) they are able to progress to investigations of familiar themes using two centre points in the room. Base A (home of Mrs A) and Base B (home of Mrs B or shop, park, school, laundry, etc.) The children will be mainly involved in the exploration which takes place in their own base site, cross linkage taking place when the children visit each other's base. This happens during the natural progression of their own group investigation. Thus Mrs A may need to visit Mrs B's home (just as neighbours visit each other in real life). Then she leaves and returns home and the two explorations continue separately until Mrs B calls on Mrs A – when reference may be made to Mrs A's visit to Home B – (perhaps Mrs A left something behind and Mrs B has returned it). The exploration may end here or Mrs B may return home and the two explorations continue again separately.

(It is useful if two portable tape recorders can be available – to record the individual investigations in the two bases – so that the children can later hear the entire exploration.)

With practice the children can explore themes which encompass two, three or more situ bases.

A group of seven year olds did in fact involve themselves in such an exploration. They began with two households and a park. The involvement grew to include two other sites unexpectedly through the development of a four site exploration which included a football ground and then five sites with the clubhouse. The children used hardly any props and began without any at first.

The households were situated at opposite ends of the room and the park in the left hand corner of the room. Only the father in one house wanted to go to the football match, as soon as the idea of football match was mentioned several boys detached themselves from the audience and began a spontaneous game of football with a ball made out of paper screwed up by a child. The audience immediately changed themselves into football fans. One boy whistled and told all the players to get under the tables and get changed. The boys pretended to dress themselves then the game recommenced. At the end of the match, the cheering died down, the players undressed and redressed themselves. Then one child invited one of the audience to come to the clubhouse. Immediately all the audience decided there was a party and everyone went to the clubhouse. To the teacher's amusement, one boy, normally quiet and a 'loner' pulled up a table and filled several jars with water which he placed on top. Asked why, he replied it was the bar. The children divided themselves into two kinds of people, dancers and drinkers, and one boy sat in the corner and pretended he was a record being played on a gramophone. The children danced to his music sounds. The barman suddenly called 'Time' and surprisingly the children began to say goodnight and departed and sat down in the far corner of the room. Only the barman was left to mop up spilt water. The improvisation had successfully ended itself, and nobody was more surprised or delighted at this achievement than the teacher.

So far the children have to some extent ordered the development of their themes by the natural flow of dialogue. During the pre-investigation discussion it was probably arranged that certain incidents would or might take place. Exactly how they were eventually included in the exploration depended entirely on the flow of the dialogue.

At this stage of work it is possible to help the children to see how they can include the incidents in a more ordered way. The children must decide on their theme, eg *The Party*. Then they work out a suitable script, ie they make a series of drawings or paintings on separate sheets of paper which depict incidents in the play. The first drawing is a picture of the home base. The second picture shows the second base. Then several intermediate drawings are made about other certain incidents.

A group of seven year olds became interested in this kind of work. One boy worked out his theme called *Buying a house*. This latter theme began with a drawing of the street where he lived. The second drawing depicted the new house which turned out to be a castle. The first intermediate drawing showed the bus on which they travelled to view the new house. The next drawing showed them walking up to the castle . . . and so on. It was particularly interesting to explore this theme with this child as he was quite imaginative. One of the intermediate drawings showed the owner of the house – 'he had one big ear and one little ear' – and it was this physical deformity on the part of the owner which conditioned the development of the theme.

The drawings were arranged into a sequence. A word script was not worked out. The conversation developed logically according to the sequence of the pictures.

The children can therefore explore fantasy themes without the themes getting out of hand.

Occasionally children should present an improvisation to an invited audience from another class, because in a sense they are strangers, visitors to the classroom (and being unfamiliar and not work mates) heighten the suspense of the performance.

58 Heidi telling a story to the class

They should work out a fairly simple two site drama exploration for this and having decided on certain incidents and characters and probable story development, they should explore their ideas, they should decide which parts and which sentences they are most particularly interested in and then a rough script should be drafted. The children now know that they are going to try to make a reasonably accurate reproduction during the first immediate investigation and that there can be no second chance to improve. Nevertheless, it will be an approximate rather than an exact word/action exploration. It must allow for slight existential changes in sentences or actions but the basic plot and the basic speech theme will remain the same. If a child forgets his exact lines it will not matter provided that he is used to making up an approximately similar sentence which will suffice and not drastically alter the main flow of the theme. This type of working to a growing script, generally prevents the investigation from becoming boring and prevents the children from developing remembered exact phrases into a sing song lilt. It also prevents a play from failing because a child forgot his lines, and missed his cue, or panicked and said lines from another part of the play which meant that part of the play was left out altogether, curtailing the length of the play and probably thus excluding several children who are no longer needed in the play – which has been known to happen when children learn a printed script from a book of school plays.

TOP INFANTS

Top infants can begin to work from instruction cards. They do not think of a theme for themselves but select a theme which interests them, from a selection of cards on which is printed some instructions which suggest an imaginary situation or incident. They are required to think about this and to make a group play which is based on the instructions.

Sometimes there may be a written extract from a story, eg *Mrs Pepperpot at the Bazaar* by Alf Proysen.

> One day Mrs Pepperpot was alone in her kitchen. At least not quite alone, because Hannah, the little girl who had the doll for Christmas, was there as well. She was busy scraping out a bowl and licking the spoon, for the old woman had been making gingerbread shapes.
>
> There was a knock at the door. Mrs Pepperpot said 'Come in'. And in walked three very smart ladies.
>
> 'Good afternoon' said the smart ladies. 'We are collecting prizes for the lottery at the school bazaar this evening. Do you think you have some little thing we could have? The money from the bazaar is for the boys' brass band – they need new instruments.'
>
> 'Oh, I'd like to help with that,' said Mrs Pepperpot, for she dearly loved brass bands. 'Would a plate of gingerbread be any use.'
>
> 'Of course,' said the smart ladies, but they laughed behind her back. 'We could take it with us now if you have it ready.' they said. But Mrs Pepperpot wanted to go to the bazaar herself, so she said she would bring the gingerbread. So the three smart ladies went away and Mrs Pepperpot was very proud and pleased that she was going to a bazaar.
>
> Hannah was still scraping away at the bowl and licking the sweet mixture off the spoon.
>
> 'May I come with you?' she asked.

The children are required to read the extract. Then to explore it in an impromptu investigation of the idea. They should invent approximate phrases for the conversation. Then older children should be encouraged to find simple extracts from literature for themselves.

59 Searching in the library for further ideas for themes

Other themes might be based on

NEWSPAPER INCIDENTS

eg In April 1969 it was reported that an American astronaut Frank Borman thought the tea cosy a South Shields couple sent him was out of this world, he wrote to thank them for the charming memento. The lady said she sent it to him because she heard he wanted an English tea cosy to take home – so she knitted him a special, blue, lemon and pink one. She said she was most thrilled to receive his letter of thanks. He said 'We are all most grateful to you and the people of England for the many courtesies you extended to me and my family during our visit'.
Read the above exercises.
Try to make an investigation into
(a) the reporter visiting the English family to discuss the news,
(b) the English family receiving letters, their reaction, etc,
(c) the reaction of Colonel Borman's family the day the tea cosy arrived.

Sometimes the children can base themes on

TAKE YOUR PICK

The class is asked to bring in pictures cut from magazines. Each picture is placed into a box. The class is divided into groups. Each member of the groups takes a picture from those mixed up in the box. The group then gather together to see what they have accidentally picked, they are required to work out a theme story that will incorporate all or most of the information given in the pictures they have selected. Each group presents its play to the others.

EXPEDITION WALKS

These often provide various incidents which can usually be explored. The class go on an expeditionary walk around the school area. They are concerned with finding incidents. The class is divided into groups. Each must find some incident which interests the whole group around which they can make up a story that will permit a valid exploration of the theme, eg on one such walk, the following events happened.

(a) A dog was lying dead in a ditch.

(b) A policeman was talking to a man a few yards up road. He was pointing his arm as though giving directions. (But were the two incidents connected?)

(c) Newspapers blew along the street.

(d) There was an exceptionally large queue of people waiting at the bus stop, when it was more usual to see only one or two people.

(e) It began to rain unexpectedly.

CONSTRUCTIONAL THEMES FOR YOUNG JUNIORS

These are themes which allow the children to make and construct something during the improvisation, eg a *Go-Kart*. The actions are based on trying to construct the actual concrete object. The incidents are concerned with finding the scrap parts etc and putting them together. The conversation develops naturally around finding the scrap or junk materials and fitting them together, although it may also allow the children to reminisce about past incidents, etc.

Older children are often required to present a play to an invited audience of parents – often at Christmas or on an open evening. Usually the chosen play is a printed script written by an author. The children are required to learn the script. This can be an ordeal for many children because they find the learning and remembering of a teacher imposed script difficult. Sometimes they are very nervous on the day of the performance and forget their lines or gesture actions. Occasionally a child may make his second speech instead of the first speech, which may un-nerve or even flummox the other children.

It is often better therefore, if the children invent their own play based on carols if it is Christmas, or songs if it is summertime. Popular songs which they hear on radio and television could be included if they are suitable. The children will suggest songs they would like to include. Then they try to make a playet around them. Some songs may not be used because an incident which would allow for their inclusion does not develop during the investigation. Sometimes they find that the songs are not really suitable and are happy to discard them. They may make several investigations and gradually discard parts which fail to develop. They learn to fit the best parts of each individual exploration together so that they finally amalgamate into a complex whole play. They do not become bored during these investigations because the play is constantly changing, evolving and growing.

Finally when they have decided on their complete play the children already know the plot, most of the words and actions. They are happy to 'polish' their performance and look forward to the final production.

MASKS

At this stage the children generally become keen to explore themes which involve the wearing of masks. This is useful because it allows investigations to be based on fantasy themes.

Most children enjoy making and wearing masks. Shy children often become proud of the mask they have made and are willing to use it to take part in an exploration. They feel perhaps that they are safely hidden behind the mask, they are thus partly freed from inhibitions.

Sometimes the masks are made because the children have thought up an idea which requires the use of masks as part of the costume. At other times they make masks during craft lessons and the finished masks suggest an idea for a theme which can be explored either in a creative dance or mime dance drama, or during a verbal improvisation. Consequently masks are extremely useful.

At first the masks can simply be a paper bag or cardboard box on which the children paint a face. These masks are quick to make, and generally suffice for an immediate spontaneous exploration. Later, as the children become more interested in mask making they can construct more elaborate ones out of junk materials. The two half sections of an egg box can be stuck together. When dry they can be painted and often look like totem faces. Hair can be made from unravelled wool, wood shavings or cut, curled paper strips which can be stapled on. A piece of elastic threaded through the sides enables the child to wear the mask.

Similarly a mask can be fashioned fairly quickly from a roll of corrugated cardboard. The sides can be stapled together. The length can be according to the individual choice of the child. Eyes are made so that the children can see. Then the basic mask is painted. When it is dry the child can decorate it with junk or natural materials according to his personal fancy. Thus a wizard's mask might have wrinkles added (made from lengths of string which is glued on). An eastern prince might be decorated with sequins, beads and silver paper. A tree sprite mask might be decorated with natural leaves and twigs.

A robot mask might be decorated simply with geometric shapes which link up with number work, ie they might have been learning how to form a three dimensional triangle or cone and this can be used as a three dimensional nose.

Larger masks can be made from chicken wire. A conical shape is made and the child covers the chicken wire with lengths of paper which are pasted on in layers. He can model the features by adding additional layers in the appropriate areas or he can have a flat smooth surface on which he can paint a face.

Masks can also be made out of *papier mâché*. A clay base is modelled and shaped. This is painted over with detergent or thin soapy liquid. Then layers of thin tissue paper are pasted on until the mask is thick and strong. This is allowed to dry. Then the child can paint it.

THE DEVELOPMENT OF A THEME

A Christmas play The theme could develop around stories based on Christmas myths or folk tales, the legend of the Christmas Rose perhaps, or it might develop around the idea of Christmas Day itself.

The theme could be explored in mime, as well as verbal drama and could include singing which would permit the parents to join in.

For example, the play could take place 'in the Round' or on stage if that is generally preferred.

The play could open with attention being focused on a decorated Christmas tree, around which are several parcels and presents. The play begins as several children enter the room and look at the Christmas tree and begin to open the parcels. The small parcels might contain a small toy, the larger boxes might contain a child actor who simulates a mechanical toy, perhaps dancing doll. She is wound up and performs a creative dance. Another box might contain wooden soldiers or puppets and they too can explore a movement sequence.

Mother and father enter and admire the toys and talk freely to the children. Singing is heard off stage. It is carol singers. They come to the house and are invited in for a wassail cup and then they sing several carols, the family join in and the audience can be invited to sing the carols as well.

As a result of singing the Christmas songs, a young child asks about Christmas and they sit down to one side of the stage or room as mother begins to explain about the Christmas Story.

During this time a group of children dressed in costumes applicable to The Nativity enter and mime out the story . . . or explore it verbally, including carols to link up the sequences, eg *While shepherds watched their flocks by night,* sung by the shepherds, *We three kings of Orient are,* sung by the travelling Wise Men, and Mary can sing selected lullabys and *The Rocking Carol* to the infant Jesus. (The parents should not be invited to sing at this stage.)

After the mime or short playlet is ended the children leave the stage or room and the play continues in the present. The carol singers leave, and the children and parents may have a meal or may go to church. In this latter case, more carols can be sung beginning with *O Come, All ye faithful.* This would lead naturally into the school carol service and the parents could stand and join in.

Thus all the children have been actively involved. They have participated according to their particular abilities in mime, verbal drama, singing and creative dance, and the parents have themselves taken an active part in the unfolding of the play. There is a sense of wholeness about the total involvement. Everyone has been needed and every part has been equally important even that of the parents.

NB If there is a good percussion band in the top class or recorder group, these could travel around with the carol singers and accompany them as they sing and thus another element could be added to the play.

Similarly, in summer, a play could be invented about a local folk tale, or actual local historical incident. The children could then explore the theme using songs of the period, or modern 'folk songs' which are suitable. The play could allow for verbal conversation, singing and poems, etc as the tale unfolds. If a festival or carnival could be included, a creative dance sequence involving a group of children could be included. Equally suitable country dances or singing games might be used. This is useful because some children have voices which do not 'carry' across a hall and they cannot be heard if they are required only to speak. If they are involved in a dance sequence they can play quite an important part. Similarly some children might be able to play in the percussion band if they represent the band playing at the carnival. Children who are adept at playing the recorder might also be able to play a simple folk tune during the course of the improvisation.

At the same time, the children can be encouraged to explore their locality to find out if buildings of the period still exist. Thus a topic can arise out of the basic play stimulus. Some children might explore architecture, others costume, food, art, transport, types of occupation and work which people engaged in and games which children played so that their knowledge becomes real and meaningful. Thus the play is the nucleus around which all the other subjects are integrated.

Through this simple concept true education can flow. It will be interesting to the children and exciting for the teacher and the work of the teacher will be constantly renewed through the originality of the children's perception.

Further reading

Language

The Lore and Language of School Children, Iona and Peter Opie, Clarendon

A Year's Course in Speech Training, Anne H. McAllister, University of London Press

Creative Power, Hugh Mearns, Dover, New York

Movement

Modern Educational Dance, Rudolf Laban revised by Lisa Ullman, MacDonald and Evans

Creative Dance in the Primary School, Joan Russell, MacDonald and Evans

Poems for Movement, E. J. M. Woodland, Evans Brothers

Personality Assessment Through Movement, Marion North, MacDonald and Evans

Drama

Stories of Improvisation, Peter Chilver, Batsford
An introduction to Child Drama, Peter Slade, University of London Press
Improvised Drama, Peter Chilver, Batsford
Talking: Discussion, Improvisation and Debate in Schools, Peter Chilver, Batsford

Puppets

The Puppet Book, Educational Puppetry Association, Faber
The Puppet, Lois H. Pratt, Stanley Paul
Folding Paper Puppets, Lewis Oppenheimer, Muller
Masks and How to Make Them, Richard Slade, Faber
Puppetry in the Primary School, David Currell, Batsford

Art

Art in the Primary School, Kay Melsi, Blackwell

Design in Nature

The Seeing Eye, Freda Lingstrom, Studio Vista
Life Under the Microscope, Jirovec, Boucek and Fiala, Spring Books
Forms and Patterns in Nature, Wolf Strache, Peter Owen
Snow Crystals, W. A. Bentley and W. J. Humphreys, Dover, New York

Education

The Problem Teacher, A. S. Neil, Jenkins
The Role of the Teacher in the Infant and Nursery Schools, Gardner and Cass, Pergamon
Young Children Living and Learning, Lilian Hollamby, Longmans
The Child and the Curriculum, J. Dewey, Phoenix University of Chicago Press

Index